The Obscure Bird

A Drama in Shakespearean Verse

by

A. K. Ludwig

Shakespeare Publications
Berkeley, California

Copyright © 2017 by A. K. Ludwig

Theatrical companies may request a free digital
copy (PDF) in play manuscript format at
Shakespeare-Publications.com.

Published by
Shakespeare Publications
Berkeley, California

ISBN-13: 978-0692946497
ISBN-10: 0692946497

For Dorothy

Preface

I wrote *The Obscure Bird: A Drama in Shakespearean Verse* for the same reasons I wrote *What's the Matter? A New Shakespeare Play*. I wanted to celebrate Shakespeare in a new way. In sampling his vast output, I wanted to provide audiences with a different opportunity to experience the dramatic verse. I wanted to make an original play composed of lines lifted from Shakespeare's works. Reshaped and pieced together, this new dialogue might serve, or even enhance, a new story and new characters in a drama that can stand on its own. However, whereas in *What's the Matter?* I tried to imitate a Renaissance drama or romance, in *The Obscure Bird* I attempt to offer a contemporary tragedy.

As I noted in the Afterword to *What's the Matter?*, within Shakespeare's works is a universe of poetic life—expressions of place, time, story, conflict, character, thought, and emotion. The theatrical world repeatedly pays homage to this accomplishment by restaging the plays with varying degrees of fidelity to the texts. In order to attract audiences to the old familiar vehicles, directors present Shakespeare in a "new" way, re-interpreting a play or characters and experimenting with staging, often to convey a personal aesthetic or political agenda (sometimes the same thing).

But there is another way to pay homage. Instead of re-interpreting the text or revamping the plot and characters of individual plays, it is possible that the treasury of poetic expression can be re-purposed. The language of the whole oeuvre can be appropriated and the lines reshuffled and given to new characters to make an original dramatic work. I still maintain that the principal reason Shakespeare endures is his inimitable use of language—the poetic expression of actions, motives, emotions, opinions, philosophies, observations of particular characters, observations on humankind, and so on—the language without which the world would not be so fascinated with Shakespeare and his creations for the past four centuries.

As with *What's the Matter?*, the entire text of *The Obscure Bird* is composed of lines selected from the plays, sonnets, and major poems in order to render Shakespeare's language in a different context, and thus provide another way to partake of its richness and vivacity. At this point, people—purists—raise the academic issue of the differences in Shakespeare's style at various stages of his dramatic career, and claim it is heresy to juxtapose lines from different periods and genres: the pentameter lines of the sonnets and extended verse works are different from the blank verse in the plays; the blank verse of 1599 and 1608 is stylistically different from the blank verse or rhyming couplets of 1592, and they are therefore incompatible; ripping lines out of context and interweaving them may subvert the play of language, or certainly not enable or render that poetic dimension.

All right—set pages of text side by side and a scholar can analyze the differences. But I am interested in the theatrical experience of hearing dialogue. Aside from recognizing many of the lines I have used in *The Obscure Bird* and *What's the Matter?*, audiences are not very likely to notice that lines circa 1595 "sound" different from lines circa 1610, and I am far from the first to slip lines from one play into another.

Besides supplying dialogue with beautiful and vigorous language, another great, intrinsic advantage to employing Shakespeare's poetic verse is that it consistently delivers invaluable dramatic benefits: it necessarily stylizes the action and conflict and heightens the expression of emotions. It not only contributes to but accounts for the force of Shakespeare's plays. I can only hope it also does so for *The Obscure Bird*, where the characters are originals, living and interacting dynamically within the drama, limited in their expression only by the speeches and lines that can be found in Shakespeare. I use the term "line" as convenient short-hand. A cursory look at *The Obscure Bird* will reveal the liberties I have taken—changing antecedents, pronouns, and the person, number, and tense of verbs to suit the speaker and occasion. Many partial lines are spliced together; sometimes single words are substituted. Sometimes extended speeches are used verbatim.

This wholesale appropriation of Shakespeare might give others—those who enjoy producing his work and reading and attending his plays for the wit and force, intimacy and reach, lyricism and grandeur of the dramatic poetry—a unique opportunity to engage with it and be entertained by it anew.

A. K. Ludwig

The Obscure Bird

Cast of Characters

<u>Arnaud</u>: The Duke, "a man of threescore years," the autocratic, tyrannical ruler of a fictional realm, with the temperament and power to bend the law to his will. He hungers sexually for his daughter-in-law, Lady Martine, and is incestuously involved with his daughter, Contessa. Martine's refusal to submit to him nearly drives him to madness, and his desire to punish her is stoked by Contessa.

<u>Martine</u>: A widow in her early 30s, grieving deeply over the recent death of her husband, Pascal. She is due to inherit all his lands and property, but her father-in-law, Arnaud, withholds her inheritance to coerce her to have sex with him. She spurns his demands and threats, even when he charges her with treason and conducts a sham hearing and trial.

<u>Contessa</u>: In her late 20s, the lascivious, conniving, unscrupulous, incestuous daughter of Duke Arnaud and the duplicitous "friend" of her sister-in-law, Martine, whom she has always resented for taking her brother from the family fold. With the power to manipulate her father, she uses his wrath and desire to punish Martine to enact her own revenge.

<u>Duplass</u>: Martine's supportive brother, about her age. He offers her any help she needs to fight the duke's charges in court, bringing in his lawyer friend Lacoste to help defend her. He suffers from self-reproach, as well as his sister's dismay, for having been involved with Contessa.

<u>Lacoste</u>: A lawyer, "of very reverend reputation; witty, courteous, liberal, full of spirit; stuffed with all honorable virtues," who assumes Martine's defense despite Arnaud's reputation for vengeance against anyone who opposes his will. In court, he must constantly restrain Martine's emotional outbursts when false charges are announced and false evidence submitted.

<u>Balthus</u>: The Lord Chief Justice, an elderly man, believed to be "a slight unmeritable man," who can be "taught and train'd and bid go forth." He claims to stand for the rule of law and is insulted by the expectation that he be Arnaud's puppet. With his position at stake, his resolve and ability to control the proceedings are tested in the trial.

Setting

A fictive feudal European duchy.

Time

An indefinite present.

Scenes

Act I

Act II

ACT I

Scene 1

*The royal residence of Duke Arnaud. An
informal meeting room. Arnaud is whispering
something to Martine; she springs away from
him and glares. He is chagrined by the rebuff
but tries to remain jocular.*

Arnaud. The dear father would with his daughter
     speak.

Martine. The more shame for you, if I were.

Arnaud. (Stepping closer to her.) Diana's lip is not
     more smooth and rubious.
          (Halting as Martine backs away.)
     I have not from your eyes that gentleness
     And show of love as I was wont to have.

Martine. (Growing more incensed.)
     Despiteful and intolerable wrongs!
     Shall I endure this monstrous villainy?

Arnaud. Why, look you, how you storm!
     I would be friends with you, and have your love.

Martine. A shameful cunning—to force that on me.
     Have you no manners? Have you no modesty?

Arnaud. Teach not thy lip such scorn, for it was made
     For kissing, lady, not for such contempt.
     God bless thee; and put meekness in thy breast;

Thou better know'st the dues of gratitude.
What have I done, that thou darst wag thy tongue
In noise so rude against me?

Martine. To reiterate were sin as deep as that.
I do condemn mine ears that have so long
Attended thee. How long shall I be patient?

Arnaud. (Suddenly charged with lust.)
My heart beats thicker than a feverous pulse.
O'er my spirit thy full supremacy thou know'st;
I dedicate myself to your sweet pleasure
And will continue fast to your affection.
For your lovely sake, say you will be mine;
Yet shall you have all kindness at my hand
That your estate requires and mine can yield.

Martine. How courtesy would seem to cover sin,
When what is done is like an hypocrite.
O Shame, where is thy blush?
Heaven's face is thought-sick at the act.

Arnaud. Rebuke me not for that which you provoke;
The offenses I make you do I'll answer.

Martine. Could such inordinate and low desires,
Such poor, such bare, such lewd, such mean
attempts,
Accompany the greatness of thy blood?
If thou wert honorable, thou wouldst not seek
Such an end. Solicit me no more.

Arnaud. If thou grant my need, by my soul I swear
I never more will break an oath with thee.

Martine. My lord, I have another oath 'gainst yours,
Of more authority, I am sure more love,

Not made in passion neither, but good heed,
That you would ne'er deny me any thing
Fit for my modest suit, and your free granting:
I tie you to your word now; if you fail in't,
Think how you maim your honor.

*Extremely agitated, Arnaud grips his head
with both hands.*

Arnaud. O ye gods, ye gods! must I endure all this?

Martine. Shall I be frighted when a madman stares?
Must I stand and crouch under your testy humor?

Arnaud. O disloyal thing, that shouldst repair my
        youth,
Thou heap'st a year's age on me.
Ingratitude, thou marble-hearted fiend!
Will it be ever thus? Ungracious wretch!

Martine. I have trusted thee, sir, but I have been
Deceived; to bide upon't, thou art not honest.

Arnaud. Silence! Cheque thy contempt: one word more
Shall make me hate thee;
Martine, I loved you, and could still,
But I must tell you, now my thoughts revolt;
Obey my will; believe not thy disdain,
Or I will throw thee from my care for ever;
Both my revenge and hate loosing upon thee,
Without all terms of pity.

Martine. (In a low seething monotone.)
Never, never, never, never, never.

Arnaud. Avaunt! be gone! thou hast set me on the rack.

Martine begins to turn and leave but sees
Arnaud gripping his head again.

Arnaud. I am exceeding weary; my mind misgives me.
My soul is heavy, and I fain would sleep.

Martine. What a sigh is there!

Arnaud. O, I have pass'd a miserable night;
I sleep in the affliction of terrible dreams.

Martine. Is it come to that? Thy heart is sorely
charged.
Unnatural deeds do breed unnatural troubles,
Infected minds; such madness rules in brainsick
men.

Arnaud. Is there no way to cure this?
Canst thou not minister to a mind diseased?

Martine. 'Tis known, I ever have studied physic,
And I can speak of the disturbances
That nature works, and of her cures.
Some griefs are med'cinable; that is one of them.

Arnaud. 'Tis you that must help me. Dearest Martine,
Raze out the written troubles of my brain
And with some sweet oblivious antidote
Cleanse the stuff'd bosom of that perilous stuff
Which weighs upon the heart.

Martine. You must be purged.

Arnaud. Thy sacred physic shall receive such pay
As thy desires can wish.

Martine. I am thus bold to put your grace in mind
　　Of what you promised me: grant my suit;
　　Keep you your word, O Duke, and that is all.

Arnaud. So! Wicked fiend! Never without your tricks!
　　I conjure thee to leave me and be gone!

Martine. Then fare you well. I leave you to your
　　　wisdom.
　　Your dreams will, sure, prove ominous to the day;
　　No medicine in the world can do thee good:
　　Not poppy, nor mandragora
　　Nor all the drowsy syrups of the world,
　　Shall ever medicine thee to that sweet sleep
　　Which thou owedst yesterday.
　　Farewell, faint-hearted and degenerate man,
　　In whose cold blood no spark of honor bides.

　　　*Exit Martine. Enter Contessa from the other
　　　side. When Arnaud rants, her responses are
　　　bemused and ironic in the manner of one who
　　　has heard this before.*

Contessa. Why, how now, Father?

Arnaud. Heard you all this?

Contessa. (Lying.) I heard nothing.

Arnaud. O miserable, unhappy that I am!
　　Wicked Martine hath struck me with her tongue,
　　Most serpent-like, upon the very heart.
　　　(Gently stroking Contessa's cheek.)
　　Dearest chuck. One only daughter have I
　　On whom I may confer what I have.
　　Ay, Contessa, my heart is drown'd with grief,
　　My mind troubled with deep melancholy;

My body round engirt with misery,
For what's more miserable than discontent?

Contessa. But what's the matter?

Arnaud. I am transform'd into a strumpet's fool;
    That witch, Martine, hast metamorphosed me.
    All the stored vengeances of heaven fall
    On her ingrateful top.
    I would she were dead at my foot.

Contessa. Your lordship is not entertained with that
    ceremonious affection as you were wont.

Arnaud. That she should refuse me!
    How bitter a thing it is, Contessa!
    I have *tremor cordis* on me; she hath tied
    Sharp-toothed unkindness, like a vulture, here.

Contessa. I cannot think Martine in the least
    Would fail her obligation.

Arnaud. A callat of boundless tongue, who now baits
        me;
    She bears herself more proudlier,
    Even to my person, than I thought she would.
    I prithee, speak to me as to thy thinkings.

Contessa. Then hear me: the terms of our estate
    May not endure hazard so near us.
    You shall do well to grant her suit
    For her husband's lands; as Martine is now
    She will but disease our better mirth;
    Take my counsel: leave your griefs; let her alone.

Arnaud. In faith, I cannot, nor I will not.

Contessa. What is't, then, Father,
     That makes you ask my opinion?

Arnaud. *(Pausing.)* Your mind is the clearer.

Contessa. Would the fountain of your mind were clear
          again.
     We'll talk when you are better temper'd.

Arnaud. *(His anger and frustration abating.)*
     Go not yet! I must not think there are
     Evils enow to darken all her goodness:
     Her faults in her seem as the spots of heaven,
     More fiery by night's blackness.
     Well may you fear too far.

Contessa. Safer than trust too far. No, no, Father,
     This milky gentleness and course of yours,
     Though I condemn it not, yet, under pardon,
     You are much more attasked for want of wisdom
     Than praised for harmful mildness.

Arnaud. I cannot speak to her. But you, Tessa—

Contessa. Say I do speak with her, then what?

Arnaud. There is hope all will be well.

Contessa. What should I say?

Arnaud. Say that upon the altar of her beauty
     I sacrifice my tears, my sighs, my heart;
     Then unfold the passion of my love.

Contessa. *(Shaking her head.)* Something else more
          plain.

Arnaud. Say, if she will take the offer of my grace,
 She'll be my friend again and I'll be hers.

Contessa. Let that suffice. Yet do I fear your nature:
 With every minute you do change your mind.

Arnaud. Please, Contessa. I do beseech you.

Contessa. As you wish. Have Joan bid her come hither.

> *Exit Arnaud. Contessa sits and looks at her
> smartphone, unhappy at what she reads there.
> Shortly, Martine enters, visibly agitated, and
> takes a seat near Contessa.*

Contessa. Why, say, Martine, what is the matter, trow?

Martine. (Wary and skeptical throughout.)
 'Tis nothing, Contessa; nothing at all.

Contessa. Whate'er it be, tell me.

Martine. When I laid my claim to my inheritance,
 I read in the duke's looks matter against me;
 And his eye reviled me, as his abject object.

Contessa. (Laughingly dismissing this.)
 You know the fiery quality of the duke;
 His disposition, all the world well knows,
 Will not be rubb'd nor stopped.
 Sister, do me the courteous office
 As to know what your offence to him is;
 It must be great that can inherit you
 So much as a thought of ill in him.

Martine. I am loath to tell you.

Contessa. Let us talk in good earnest. Is it possible,
　　　On such a sudden, you and he should fall
　　　Into so strong a quarrel?

Martine. Ay, it is possible enough.

Contessa. Sure he misconstrues whatever you have
　　　done.

Martine. I have done nothing but say "no" to his
　　　demand.

Contessa. But he is thy lord, thy life, thy sovereign;
　　　Such duty as the subject owes the prince
　　　Even a woman oweth to her father.

Martine. Your father.
　　　I know no touch of consanguinity.
　　　　　(Aside.)
　　　And so unnatural a father.

Contessa. Indeed. Yet in this life, men
　　　Are masters to their females, and their lords:
　　　I am ashamed that women are so simple
　　　To offer war where they should kneel for peace,
　　　When they are bound to serve, love, and obey.

Martine. Good faith, I wish'd myself a man,
　　　Or that we women had men's privileges.

Contessa. What does my father lay to Martine's charge?

Martine. To perform his bidding, on pain of perpetual
　　　Displeasure. Nothing more.

Contessa. Alack, what heinous sin is it in me
　　　To be ashamed to be my father's child?

His temper must be well observed;
Chide him for faults, but do it reverently,
When you see his blood inclined to mirth;
With all gracious utterance that thou hast,
Speak to his gentle hearing kind commends;
But, being moody, give him time and scope
Till that his passions, like a whale on ground,
Confound themselves with working.

Martine. I never heard a passion so confused.

Contessa. What he cannot help in his nature, you
Account a vice in him; rather, impute his words
To wayward sickliness and age in him.
So let your will attend on his accords;
He loves you, on my life, and holds you dear.
I shall observe him with all care and love,
Till he be dieted to my request,
And then I'll set upon him. I'll entreat for thee;
What I can do I will; and more I will
Than for myself I dare. You must be patient:
Time serves wherein you may restore yourself
Into the good thoughts of the duke again.

Martine. I will be patient, if he will grant my suit.

Contessa. His eyes must with my judgment look.

Martine. (Still warily.) I thank you, Contessa. I am in
your debt.

*Martine prepares to stand and depart.
Contessa pauses and regards her. Martine
settles again in her seat.*

Contessa. Tarry a little; there is something else;
I beg some private speech with you.

Martine. Yes?

> *Contessa suddenly kneels in front of Martine,*
> *takes her hands, and holds them in Martine's*
> *lap.*

Contessa. I durst commend a secret to your ear:
I am horribly in love with Duplass.

Martine. My brother? These are news indeed!

Contessa. I love him beyond love and beyond reason,
Or wit, or safety: I have made him know it.
(Pulling out her smartphone and shaking it.)
Now he spurns my love.

Martine. Why do you speak to me?

Contessa. I shall desire your help, Martine;
What shall I do to win Duplass again?

Martine. Why do you wring your hands?

Contessa. My state is desperate for his love:
I know not how I lost him. Here I kneel:
If e'er my will did trespass 'gainst his love,
Either in discourse of thought or actual deed,
Or that I do not love him dearly,
Comfort forswear me! Unkindness may do much;
And his unkindness may defeat my life.
Speak to him, see if you can move him.
Be eloquent in my behalf.

Martine. Well, I will see what I can do for you.

Blackout.

ACT I

Scene 2

*In the same room, somewhat later, Arnaud
awaits Martine. She enters and bows. He
gestures for her to come closer.*

Martine. Duke Arnaud, my ingratitude even now
   Is heavy on me;
   And I have learn'd me to repent the sin
   Of disobedient opposition;
   I beseech your lordship to make it
   Natural rebellion, too strong for reason's force,
   And do entreat thou pardon me my wrongs.

Arnaud. Come hither, gentle mistress. Do you
   Perceive where most you owe obedience?

Martine. My life and education both do learn me
   How to respect you: you are the lord of duty.

Arnaud. (Affectionately.)
   Relenting fool, and shallow, changing woman,
   Thou hast redeemed thy lost opinion.
   I here forget all former griefs, cancel all grudge,
   And drown the sad remembrance of those wrongs
   Which thou supposest I have done to thee.

Martine. Supposest?
      (Aside, tamping down her rising outrage.)
   O, constancy, be strong upon my side.

Arnaud. With my nobler reason 'gainst my fury
    Do I take part; thou being penitent,
    All is whole.

Martine. (Swallowing her outrage.)
    Thou shalt find that I'll resume the shape which
    Thou dost think I have cast off.

Arnaud. And, since I saw thee,
    The affliction of my mind amends, with which,
    I fear, a madness held me.

Martine. To leave thee in thy madness, 'twere my sin.
    I should have found some way
    To ease the gnawing vulture of thy mind
    That was thy cause of anger.

Arnaud. Lay not that flattering unction to your soul
    That not your trespass but my madness spoke.

Martine. Once again, I beseech thee pardon me.

Arnaud. Now no discourse, except it be of love:
    'Tis pity that we make our faces vizards
    To our hearts, disguising what they are.
    If I be false, or swerve a hair from truth,
    When time is old and hath forgot itself,
    When mighty states characterless are gated
    To dusty nothing, yet let memory
    Upbraid my falsehood!

Martine. As I believe thee, and humbly thank thee,
    May I now beseech thee to grant one boon?

Arnaud. What shall you ask of me that I'll deny?

From her jacket pocket, Martine pulls two
small, framed, keepsake photos, looks at
one, and shows it to Arnaud.

Martine. I have bewept a worthy husband's death,
    And lived by looking on his images:
    A man whom fortune hath cruelly scratched.

Arnaud. So I have lost—how sharp the point
    Of this remembrance is!—my dear son.

Martine. So came I a widow:
    And never shall have length of life enough
    To rain upon remembrance with mine eyes.

Martine shows Arnaud the other photo.

Martine. Look here upon my husband Pascal's face;
    These eyes, these brows, were molded out of yours.
    You to him engaged a father's word
    To do me all the grace and good you could.
    Now liberty is all that I request,
    That I may have welcome and free access
    To my husband's lands.

Arnaud. (Flirtatiously.)
    I'll tell you how these lands are to be got.

Martine. So shall you bind me to your highness'
        service.

Arnaud. What service wilt thou do me, if I give them?

Martine. What you command, that rests in me to do,
    Except I cannot do it.

Arnaud. Ay, but thou canst do what I mean to ask.

Martine. Why, then I will do what your grace
    commands.

Arnaud. An easy task; 'tis but to love your duke.

Martine. That's soon performed, because I am his
    subject.

Arnaud. Why, then thy husband's lands I freely give
    thee.

Martine. I take my leave with many thousand thanks.

Arnaud. What love think'st thou I sue so much to get?

Martine. My love till death, my humble thanks, my
    prayers;
    That love which virtue begs and virtue grants.

Arnaud. No, by my troth, I did not mean such love.
    But now you partly may perceive my mind.

Martine. I am sorry that I am deceived in you;
    My mind will never grant what I perceive.

Arnaud. Why, then thou shalt not have thy husband's
    lands.

Martine. *(Tying to make light of this sexual extortion.)*
    This merry inclination, Duke Arnaud,
    Accords not with the sadness of my suit;
    Please you dismiss me either with "ay" or "no."

Arnaud. Ay, if thou wilt say "ay" to my request;
    No if thou dost say "no" to my demand.

Martine. Then no, my lord. My suit is at an end.

Arnaud. *(Suddenly enraged.)* Ingrateful creature!
    You spurn me like a cur out of your way!
    With thy contempt I am struck to the quick.

Martine. I am sorry that I run in your displeasure.

Arnaud. Martine, as you look to have my pardon,
    If you will perform my bidding
    Your trespass shall be well forgot.

Martine. I beseech your grace: let me know my trespass
    By its own visage.

Arnaud. You well know, disobedient wretch!

Martine. Treacherous man; thou hast beguiled my
      hopes.
    What would you have me be? A whore?

Arnaud. *(Turning slightly manic with lust.)*
    Who lives that's not depraved or depraves?
    It is a bawdy planet, that will strike
    Where 'tis predominant; and 'tis powerful!

Martine. Boundless intemperance in nature is a
      tyranny.
    Thou subtle, perjured, false, disloyal man!

Arnaud. *(Becoming giddy with desire.)*
    Let copulation thrive!
    As we are human, thus should we do;
    No barricado for a belly;
    To't, luxury, pell-mell!
    Be not like yon simpering dame,
    Whose face between her forks presages snow;
    That minces virtue, and does shake the head
    To hear of pleasure's name;

The wren goes to't, and the small gilded fly
Does lecher in our sight;
The fitchew, nor the soiled horse, goes to't
With more riotous appetite.

*Laughing, Arnaud reaches with a finger to set a
lock of hair behind her ear, but she withdraws.*

Arnaud. It would grieve an able man to leave
  So sweet a bedfellow.

Martine. Shall I be tempted of the devil thus?
  I will not be your . . . I cannot say "whore":
  It does abhor me now to speak the word.
  Take my defiance! I despise thee!

Arnaud. Evermore cross'd and cross'd, nothing but
      crossed!
  The hearts of princes kiss obedience,
  So much they love it; but to stubborn spirits
  They swell, and grow as terrible as storms.
  I'll tame you; I'll bring you in subjection;
  Either frame your will to mine and be ruled
  By me, or I will make you.

Martine. Never! So will I die ere I will yield.

Arnaud. Let me put in your mind, if you forget,
  What you have been ere this, and what you are;
  Withal, what I have been, and what I am.
  Thou must needs be sure
  My spirit and my place have in them power
  To make this bitter to thee;
  Come not within the measure of my wrath.
  Look to it well and say you are well warned.

Martine. I must offend before I be attainted;
        And I never did offend thee in my life;
        My lord, I am loyal, true, and crimeless.
        Tender my suit, I heartily beseech thee.

Arnaud. But you take exceptions to my boon;
        And for your offence I will be deaf
        To pleading and excuses; therefore use none.

Martine. Thou shalt have none, for I made no offence.
        If it please thee, dismiss me hence.

Arnaud. Leave me. Your mind perhaps may change;
        For this time, though full of my displeasure,
        Yet I free thee from the dead blow of it.
        Do as thou wilt, for I have done with thee.
        Thou art obdurate, flinty, hard as steel,
        Nay, more than flint, for stone at rain relenteth;
        Art thou a woman born, and canst not feel
        What 'tis to love? How want of love tormenteth?
        I prithee, Martine, do not make me mad.

        *Arnaud grips the sides of his head as Martine
                        retreats.*

Martine. Yet again? Brainsick, degenerate man:
        You lack the season of all natures, sleep—
        Balm of hurt minds, great nature's second course—
        To repair your self with comforting repose
        And ease you of your griefs; never shall you
        Enjoy the honey-heavy dew of slumber.
        The time will come when you shall wish for me
        To help you cure your brains and your
        Desperate languishings. I take my leave.

        Exit Martine. Arnaud shouts in her direction.

Arnaud. Now do I wish it! Cure me of this evil!
    Cure this great breach in my abused nature!
    Fie, fie upon her! she's able to freeze the god
    Priapus, and undo a whole generation!

      Contessa enters unnoticed behind him and
              stands listening.

Arnaud. Hysterica passio, down!
      (Pause.)
    The more she spurns my love,
    The more it grows and fawneth on her still;
    When to her beauty I commend my vows,
    She twits me with my falsehood,
    And bids me think how I have been forsworn.
    Merciful powers,
    Restrain in me the cursed thoughts that nature
    Gives way to in repose.

      Contessa approaches and places a hand on
              his shoulder.

Contessa. Come, sir, come, sir.

Arnaud. Contessa! My dearest!
    I am vanquished; these haughty words of hers
    Have batter'd me like roaring cannon-shot;
    She shall rue this treason with her tears.
    I will have an apology.

Contessa. Why, what a wasp-stung and impatient fool
    Art thou to break into this woman's mood.
    I would you would make use of your good wisdom
    Whereof I know you are fraught.

Arnaud. (Still wound up.) Like the hectic in my blood
    she rages!

Contessa. Say that she were gone—a moiety of your rest
    Might come to you again.

Arnaud. (Still wound up.) One way or other, she is for
    me.

Contessa. My dearest lord, put away
    These dispositions that of late transform you
    From what you rightly are. You do unbend
    Your noble strength, to think so brainsickly.
    Listen to me; take my counsel:
    It would better fit your honor to change
    Your mind. You do not know her, as I do:
    To your high person her will is most malignant;
    She does disdain you much beyond your thoughts.

Arnaud. Which makes me sweat with wrath. She hath
        despis'd
    Me rejoicingly, and I'll be merry
    In my revenge.

Contessa. She never loved you, only affected
    Greatness got by you, as wife to your son.
    She hath bought the name of whore thus dearly.

Arnaud. Yet your brother did love her.

Contessa. Doth it therefore ensue that she should love
        you?
    And as for Pascal, let me be cruel:
    When he was dear to us, we did hold him so.
    That a brother should
    Be so perfidious!—he whom next thyself
    Of all the world I loved, did betray us.
    So I do wash his name out of my blood.

Arnaud. You allay my rages and revenges with
　　Your colder reasons.

Contessa. I have a brain that leads my use of anger
　　To better vantage: I'd give you a further edge
　　And drive your purpose on.
　　'Tis policy and stratagem must do
　　That you affect; and so must you resolve,
　　That what you cannot as you would achieve,
　　You must perforce accomplish as you may.

Arnaud. I will conclude to hate her, nay, indeed,
　　To be revenged upon her.

Contessa. We shall make those that do offend you
　　　　suffer,
　　And all things shall redound unto your good.

Blackout.

ACT I

Scene 3

*Some days later. A sitting room in the home
of Martine's brother, Duplass. Martine sits,
elbows on armrests, head in hands. Duplass
enters.*

Duplass. How now, dear sister?

Martine. Sure, you have heard the news abroad,
    Duplass:
Duke Arnaud denies me my husband's lands.

Duplass. Ay.

Martine. Still worse, he would seduce me to his
    shameful lust.

Duplass. Damned lecherous villain.

Martine. He hearkens after prophecies and dreams;
These, as I learn, and such like toys as these,
Have moved his lordship to indict me now,
Assisted by Contessa, a very fiend—
A most wicked, cunning fiend.

Duplass. (Uneasy at the mention of Contessa.)
Prithee, be not sad.

Martine. To be called a whore—would it not make one
    weep?
I cannot but be sad. So heavy sad.

Thou knowst my main grief springs from the loss
Of a beloved husband, basely slain;
Falsely murder'd. O, untimely death!

Duplass. You must not think . . .

Martine. His means of death, his obscure funeral—
No noble rite nor formal ostentation—
Cry to be heard, as 'twere from heaven to earth,
That I must call't in question.

Duplass. No, no, they would not do so foul a deed.
Witness the sorrow that Contessa makes.

Martine. If that the earth could teem with woman's
tears
Each drop she falls would prove a crocodile.

Duplass. Do not seek to take your charge upon you,
To bear your griefs yourself and leave me out.

Martine. Then think upon my grief, a lady's grief;
Assist me, dear brother!
Do but say to me what I should do
That in your knowledge may by me be done,
And I am prest unto it.

Duplass. Oppose yourself against the duke:
Challenge him by law.

Martine. How?

Duplass. By attorney. I'll call Monsieur Lacoste.
        (Dialing a number on his cell phone.)
Lacoste. Duplass. You are hotly called for.
        (Pause.)
Even on the instant.

(Pause.)
I'll see you soon.
    (He puts away his phone.)
Be assured, my dear sister,
My purse, my person, my extremest means,
Lie all unlock'd to your occasions.

Martine. But I say there is no hope.
    The duke will suspect you and find a time
    To punish this offence in other faults.

Duplass. Go to; let that be mine.
    Lacoste is a grave and noble counsellor;
    He hath a prone and speechless dialect,
    Such as moves men; and he hath prosperous art
    When he will play with reason and discourse,
    And well he can persuade.

Martine. (Lengthy pause.)
    Duplass, Contessa spoke to me;
    I am solicited—

        Duplass is taken aback at the mention of
            Contessa. He cuts her off.

Duplass. I can guess; this does not please me.

Martine. I confess, I knew nothing,
    Nor ever heard, nor ever did suspect.

Duplass. I would you knew nothing more.

Martine. Then Duke Arnaud and you both are rivals.

Duplass. (Shocked at what she knows.)
    I would not have you know so much.

Martine. But doth he know?

Duplass. (Shaking his head "no.") Ignorant.

Martine. Keep it so.

Duplass. Would you were so too.

Martine. Be wary; best safety lies in fear:
 To keep his bed of blackness unlaid ope,
 He'd make pretense of that you have done him
 By direct and indirect attempts.
 Duplass, why Contessa? She is subtle,
 False, and treacherous. You cannot love her.

Duplass. I have loved her since first I saw her;
 And still I see her beautiful;
 Her face was to mine eye beyond all wonder;
 The rest, by my knowledge, as black as incest;
 There's no bottom, none, in her voluptuousness—
 One that knows what she should shame to know
 But with her most vile principal; one that
 Sleeps in the contriving of lust and wakes
 To do the deed of darkness and commit
 The oldest sins the newest kind of ways.

Martine. Sick fool, whom love hath turned almost
 The wrong side out.

Duplass. Shameful it is; ay, if the fact be known:
 It is a lust of the blood; lechery;
 Which ever since hath kept my eyes from rest;
 For never yet one hour in her bed
 Did I enjoy the golden dew of sleep.
 She is a disease in my flesh; a boil,
 A plague-sore in my corrupted blood.
 I must tell you, now my gorge rises at it.

I banished her my bed and company.
If ere I loved her, all that love is gone.

Martine. Bad child; worse father.

> *Enter Lacoste. Duplass stands and they*
> *shake hands.*

Duplass. Ah, Lacoste. Most welcome, sir.

Lacoste. You required my haste-post-haste appearance.

Duplass. The need we have to use you did provoke
Our hasty sending. My sister, Lady Martine.

> *Lacoste bows to Martine and takes her*
> *extended hand and kisses it.*

Lacoste. Madam. At your service.

Martine. I greet thee well, Monsieur Lacoste,
And thank you for the great favor.

> *Duplass and Lacoste sit on either side of*
> *Martine.*

Duplass. Bold of your worthiness, we single you
As our best-moving fair solicitor.

Lacoste. I'll do for thee what I can. What's the quarrel?

Duplass. I can tell you that of late Duke Arnaud
Hath taken displeasure against Martine;
And on my life, his malice 'gainst the lady
Will suddenly break forth.

Lacoste. I must confess that I have heard so much.

Martine. The net has fall'n upon me. I shall perish
   Under device and practice.

Duplass. He seeks revenge and therefore will not yield;
   If law and authority deny not
   It will go hard with poor Martine.

Lacoste. Arnaud cannot deny the course of law.
   Though he doth sway the rule awhile,
   The state takes notice of the private difference
   Betwixt you and the duke.

Martine. I advise you to consider further that
   What his high hatred would effect wants not
   A minister in his power;
   None serve with him but constrained things.

Lacoste. Indeed, who knows not so?
   I doubt some danger does approach you nearly.
   I will be attorney'd at your service.

Martine. 'Tis a cause less promising
   Than a wild dedication of yourself
   To unpath'd waters, undream'd shores.
   Beware, Lacoste, if thou dost plead for me
   Thou wilt but add increase unto his wrath.
   Can you think that any man
   Dare give me counsel? Or be a known friend,
   'Gainst the duke's pleasure, and live a subject?
   All continent impediments he will
   O'erbear that do oppose his will.
   Take heed, for he holds vengeance in his hands,
   To hurl upon their heads that break his law.

Lacoste. I know what his reputation is.

Martine. (Musing.) Methinks, I could be well content
    To be my own attorney in this case.
    I will practice the insinuating nod.

Lacoste. There is a thing within my bosom tells me
    You should not.

Martine. There is a fair behavior in thee, Lacoste;
    I will believe thou hast a mind that suits
    With this thy fair and outward character.
    To your protection I commend me, sir;
    Step forth mine advocate,
    And out of thy long-experienced time,
    Bestow your needful counsel
    How with my honor I may undertake
    To oppose the duke.

Lacoste. This shall I undertake with all my heart.
    Now, to the bottom of your story.

Martine. For my dowry, Pascal assur'd me of
    My widowhood, be it that I survived him,
    In all his lands and leases whatsoever.

Lacoste. And what says Duke Arnaud?

Martine. He swore to me that he did hold me dear,
    Adding thereto deep oaths of his deep kindness.
    But he hath broke his solemn oaths:
    He doth lay claim to mine inheritance;
    And he will not yield my husband's lands.

Lacoste. Let us prepare.
    I will send the Lord Chief Justice
    The parcels and particulars of your griefs.

Ere I part from thee, I beseech you,
If you know aught which does behove my
     knowledge
Thereof to be inform'd, imprison't not
In ignorant concealment.

Blackout.

ACT I

Scene 4

*A short time after. The duke's official meeting
chamber. Arnaud is seated at a large desk.
Contessa enters and sits opposite.*

Contessa. I have summon'd Lord Chief Justice Balthus.

Arnaud. Are his wits safe? Is he not light of brain?

Contessa. He shall suffice. You shall see anon.

> *Contessa signals. Balthus enters and waits
> before sitting.*

Arnaud. How now, my Lord Chief Justice!

Balthus. (Bowing.) Good day to both your graces.

Contessa. Your honor.

> *Arnaud gestures for Balthus to take a seat
> and looks to Contessa for further cues.*

Arnaud. Lord Balthus, you are come to advise me;
   It concerns the Lady Martine de Luc.

Balthus. Your daughter-in-law?

Arnaud. The very truth is that, she hath wronged me,
   Given me most egregious indignity,
   And—

Contessa impatiently interrupts to refine
Arnaud's point.

Contessa. To gorge her distempered appetite
          She hath resisted law and the duke's will,
          And her offence is so, as it appears,
          Accountant to the law.

Balthus. There is a law in each well-order'd nation
          To curb those raging appetites that are
          Most disobedient and refractory.

Arnaud. I beg the ancient privilege of office:
          As she is mine, I may dispose of her
          According to the law
          Immediately provided in the case.

Balthus. But let my counsel sway you; pause awhile—

Arnaud. (*Aside.*) I knew he was not in his perfect wits.

Balthus. This I will advise you: and this will I do:
          Look into this business thoroughly,
          Call the Lady Martine to her answers,
          And poise the cause in justice's equal scales,
          Whose beam stands sure, whose rightful cause
               prevails.

Contessa. The lady is disloyal.

Balthus. Her faults lie open to the laws; let them,
          Not you, correct her.

Arnaud. She will have no attorney but herself.

Contessa. Monsieur Lacoste is attorney'd at her service.

Arnaud. Who is this? How is the man esteemed here?

Balthus. Of very reverend reputation, sir.
    Second to none that lives here in the city;
    Witty, courteous, liberal, full of spirit;
    Stuffed with all honorable virtues;
    As pregnant in the terms for common justice
    As art and practice had enriched any.

Arnaud. We decree she will have no attorney.

Balthus. I know your lordship would not deny her what
    A woman of less place might ask by law:
    Scholars allow'd freely to argue for her.

Arnaud. Is that the law?

Balthus. Yes, it is the law. To deny it her,
    By law and process, you must provide
    A reason mighty, strong, and effectual;
    A pattern and precedent to perform the like.

Arnaud. Make thine own edict for thy pains, which we
    Will answer as a law.

Balthus. *(Demurring.)* All must be even in our
      government,
    Keeping law and form and due proportion.

Arnaud. What, will you not do as I command you?

Balthus. *(Cowed.)* I am loath to break our country's
      laws;
    (Pausing after seeing Contessa's glare.)
    However, my lord, this I'll do for you:
    Though we may not pass upon her life

Without the form of justice, yet our power
Shall do a courtesy to your wrath.

Arnaud. And you shall find yourself to be well thank'd.

Contessa. What pledge have we of thy firm loyalty?

Balthus. (Insulted.) None, your grace. I am accountant
    to the law.
Be it known to you, I do remain as neuter.

Arnaud. It well befits you should be, Lord Balthus.
Enough, Contessa. I am satisfied.

Contessa. Prepare you, then, good my Lord Chief
    Justice;
Summon a session, that we may arraign
This most disloyal lady.

Balthus. As she hath been publicly accused,
So she shall have a just and open trial.

    Balthus rises, bows to both, and exits.

Arnaud. This is a slight unmeritable man,
    Meet to be sent on errands;
He must be taught and train'd and bid go forth.

Contessa. And now, dear Father, you know my
    meaning.

    Blackout.

ACT I

Scene 5

*Some days later. A formal hearing chamber.
Upstage center are a desk and chair on a dais; to
its left and right, extending diagonally downstage,
are two long tables; each with chairs on one side;
each set of chairs faces the other across the stage.
Lacoste, Duplass, and Martine enter, pausing
before sitting.*

Lacoste.   Lord Chief Justice Balthus hath sent to know
     The nature of your griefs.
     He will give ear to your complaint
     And give you justice. Let us go in
     And charge us there upon inter'gatories.
        (Aside to Martine.)
     Good now, play one scene
     Of excellent dissembling; and let it look
     Like perfect honor; entertain good comfort,
     And cheer his grace with quick and merry words;
     Make thy will the advantage of thy good,
     So far as thou hast power and person,
     And thou wilt frame thyself hereafter theirs,
     That thou mayst enjoy thy husband's lands.

*Lacoste, Duplass, and Martine take seats at
one table, the men flanking her. Arnaud and
Contessa enter and sit at the other table,
facing them. Balthus enters and sits on the
dais. Lacoste, Martine, and Duplass rise.*

Balthus.   Welcome, Lady Martine, and gentlemen.

Duplass and *Lacoste. (Bowing.)*
    Lord Chief Justice Balthus.

Martine. (Curtseying.) In all submission and humility,
    I present myself unto your grace.

Arnaud. (Softly at the sight of Martine.)
    How lovely! By God, she's beautiful!

Contessa. (Giving Arnaud a look of annoyance.)
    When devils will the blackest sins put on,
    They do suggest at first with heavenly shows.

Balthus. (Indicating they should sit.)
    I have labored to bring you and the duke
    Unto this bar and royal interview;
    I bid you name your griefs, and wherein
    It shall appear that your demands are just,
    You shall enjoy redress of these same grievances;
    Relate your wrongs; in what? by whom? Be brief.

Martine. (Excitedly.) O Chief Justice Balthus, vail your
        regard
    Upon a wrong'd woman! I have suffered
    Wrongs unspeakable, past patience,
    More than any living woman could bear.

Balthus. Calmly, madam, I do beseech you.
    What is that wrong whereof you here complain?

Martine. (Aside, struggling with her emotions.)
    O, constancy,
    Set a huge mountain 'tween my heart and tongue.

Duplass. Sir, since the loss of her husband, most retired
    Hath her life been; the cure whereof, my lord,
    'Tis time must do. I beseech your honor,

Forbear sharp speeches to her. She's a lady
So tender of rebukes that words are strokes
And strokes death to her.

Martine begins to weep.

Balthus. Alas the heavy day! Why do you weep?

Martine. Perchance because they kill'd my husband.

Arnaud. You are mad. My lord, her wits, I fear me,
Are not firm. Let me speak, sir.

Martine. (Collecting herself, to Balthus.)
My lord, neglect me not, with that opinion
That I am touched with madness
Till you have heard me in my true complaint,
And given me justice. Justice!

Balthus. Be't so. Have patience, noble duke. Proceed.

Martine. A heavy heart bears not a nimble tongue.
To be brief, my lord, the very truth is that
For my dowry, upon his death, Pascal
By will bequeath'd his lands to me.
The duke swore consent to my succession;
But when I laid claim to my inheritance,
The duke reft'st me of my lands, and all things
That I do call mine he seized into his hands.
I told him gently of my grievances,
And his oath-breaking; which he mended thus:
An oath is of no moment, being not took
Before a true and lawful magistrate
That hath authority over him that swears;
He in rage dismissed me from the court,
And in conclusion play'd foul with his oaths,

Which he broke as easily as tearing paper.
By this means Duke Arnaud hath wronged me.

Arnaud. This is mere falsehood! I'll see thee damned.
The sessions shall proceed with indictment!

Lacoste. My Lord Chief Justice! Hold, hold!
'Tis contrary to form of law!

Balthus. Not now, not now, Duke Arnaud.

Martine. (Shouting.) Tell me wherein I have offended.
Whom have I injured?

Lacoste. (Sternly to Martine.)
Speak not you to *him* till I call upon you.

> *While Lacoste speaks to Martine, Arnaud,*
> *taking a cue from Contessa, stands and*
> *shakes a sheaf of papers at Martine.*

Arnaud. I have the summary of all our griefs,
When time shall serve, to show in articles.

Lacoste. Lord Balthus, the duke is most out of order!

Balthus. Sir, proceed no further in this business.

Arnaud. (To Martine, raising his voice, ignoring
Lacoste and Balthus.)
Little faults, proceeding on distemper,
May be wink'd at;
But mightier crimes are laid to your charge,
Whereof you cannot easily purge yourself:
Capital crimes, chew'd, swallow'd, and digested.

Lacoste. Chief Justice, I do protest!

Balthus. Duke Arnaud, prithee, no more; cease;
    On height of our displeasure.

Martine. *(To Arnaud.)* You speak a language that I
        understand not;
    Senseless speaking or a speaking
    Such as sense cannot untie.
    My life stands in the level of your dreams.

      While Martine speaks to Arnaud, Lacoste
      grimaces in dismay and puts a hand on
            Martine's arm.

Arnaud. Your actions are my dreams.

Martine. You cannot produce more accusation
    Than your own weak-hinged fancy;
    This is the very coinage of your brain.
    He speaks nothing but madman; fie on him!
    O, you blessed ministers above,
    Keep me in patience, and with ripen'd time
    Unfold the evil which is here wrapt up
    In countenance!

Arnaud. *(With a prompt from Contessa.)*
    Hark thee! Chief Justice Balthus: note well
    This supernatural soliciting!

Lacoste. *(Aside to Duplass.)*
    All in vain comes counsel to her ear. Dost
    Thou think in time she will let instruction
    Enter where folly now possesses?

Duplass. What her heart thinks her tongue speaks.

Balthus. Peace! Duke, sit you down. Lady Martine,
    peace!

Arnaud sits down.

Martine. (Half to herself.) I am amazed, methinks, and
    lose my way
Among the thorns and dangers of this world.
I have done no harm. But I remember now
I am in this earthly world; where to do harm
Is often laudable, to do good sometime
Accounted dangerous folly: why then, alas,
Do I put up that womanly defense,
To say I have done no harm?
O give me strength, and innocence shall make
False accusation blush and tyranny
Tremble at patience.
    (To Arnaud.)
What studied torments, tyrant, hast for me?
What wheels? racks? fires? what flaying? boiling?
In leads or oils? what old or newer torture
Must I receive, whose every word deserves
To taste of thy most worst?

Lacoste. Lady Martine, I beg of thee.

Arnaud. *(On his feet again; outraged.)*
    Dost thou call me "tyrant"?

Martine. I do, most heartily.

Arnaud. For your life you durst not!

Martine. And I shall. Hear me this:
    (Looking at Contessa.)
Though I partly know the instrument
That screws me from my true place in your favor,
Live you the tyrant still.

Arnaud. This session even pushes 'gainst our heart:
    Let us be clear'd
    Of being tyrannous, since we so openly
    Proceed in justice, which shall have due course,
    Even to the guilt or the purgation;
    So we shall proceed without suspicion.

Duplass. Under your hard construction must she sit?

Balthus. Quiet yourselves, I pray, and be at peace!

Lacoste. Lord Chief Justice,
    Is this proceeding just and honorable?

Arnaud. (Shouting.) The session shall proceed!

Lacoste. (Standing and shuffling side to side.)
    Lord Chief Justice, how is this justified?
    How is this deriv'd? How is this "due course"?
    You promis'd to give ear to her complaint.
    I must entreat you, sir; grant us justice.

      Rattled, Balthus rises, puts his hands on the
             desk, and leans across.

Balthus. Counsellor, you shall be satisfied.

Lacoste. It doth impeach the freedom of the state
    If you deny us justice.

Balthus. Be assured thou shalt have justice, sir.
    In the mean time, 'tis a needful fitness
    That we adjourn this court for a while.

      All push back their chairs. Contessa rises,
      goes to Martine, and places a hand on her

*shoulder in sympathy. Arnaud and Balthus
observe. Lacoste and Duplass huddle.*

Martine. (Shrugging off Contessa's hand.)
 What, was I born to this, that my sad look
 Should grace the triumph of sly Contessa?
 Why dost thou wrong her that did ne'er wrong thee?
 When did I ever cross thee with a bitter word?

Contessa. Didst thou speak with Duplass? Knowst thou
 his mind?

Martine. Doubt it not, he does abhor thee.

*Contessa. (In a measured tone, after regarding
 Martine a long moment.)*
 Ah, dear Martine, I grieve at what I speak;
 I have, and most unwillingly, of late
 Heard many grievous, I do say, Martine,
 Grievous complaints of you.
 Trust me, were it not against my father,
 My soul should sue as advocate for thee.

Martine. Tut, tut, you said so much before.
 I must no more believe thee in this point
 Than I will trust a sickly appetite,
 That loathes even as it longs.
 No visor does become black villainy
 So well as soft and tender flattery.

Contessa. Lady, I want that glib and oily art,
 To speak and purpose not.

Martine. I do know your spirit. I do not like you,
 And will not trust one of your malice.

Contessa. And you, Martine, you that didst set up
          Your disobedience 'gainst the duke my father—
          You play the pious innocent:
          You sign your place and calling, in full seeming,
          With meekness and humility; but your heart
          Is cramm'd with arrogancy, spleen, and pride.

Martine. What devil art thou, that dost torment me
              thus,
          And bait me with this foul derision?

Contessa. Do not presume too much upon my love;
          I may do that I shall be sorry for.

Martine. You have done that you should be sorry for.
          Contessa, I know you what you are:
          As duteous to the vices of the duke
          As badness would desire.
          You have an angel's face, but heaven knows your
              heart;
          You hide a thousand daggers in your thoughts.

Contessa. You have no cause to hold my friendship
              doubtful:
          I never was nor never will be false.

Martine. Dissembling harlot! thou art false in all!
          Causeless have you laid disgraces on my head,
          And blown this coal betwixt the duke and me;
          Heaven truly knows that thou art false as hell.
          Thou disease of a friend.

Contessa. (Pityingly.) I look on you as one that takes
              her leave;
          We'll bar you from succession;
          Not hold thee of our blood, no, not our kin.

Martine. But thou hast already! So fare thee well,
Most foul, most fair! farewell; friendship, blood,
And all the ties between us I disclaim.

Contessa. (With a mixture of threat and pity.)
For now, fair sister, look you arm yourself
To fit your fancies to my father's will;
'Twill be much
Both for your honor better and your cause;
For if the trial of the law o'ertake you,
You'll part away disgraced. Be advised.

> *Contessa moves from Martine to Duplass,*
> *still huddled with Lacoste; she waits till he*
> *reluctantly acknowledges her presence.*
> *Lacoste turns away.*

Duplass. Contessa.

Contessa. Duplass.

> *Contessa indicates that they should move*
> *away from the table. She steps downstage.*
> *Duplass follows. She crowds him face-to-*
> *face. Martine and Lacoste observe.*

Duplass. You throw a strange regard upon me.

Contessa. (Softly.) Let us speak our free hearts each to
other.

Duplass. Why dost thou so oppress me with thine eye?

Contessa. Come, I know thou lovest me.

Duplass. I can no longer.

Contessa. Dost thou affect another? I prithee now, with
      most petitionary vehemence, *tell me who it is!*
            (Duplass does not answer.)
      Your lips to mine how often hath you joined,
      Between each kiss your oaths of true love swearing!
      But sweet love, I see, changing his property,
      Turns to the sourest and most deadly hate.
            (Pause.)
      Do you love your sister?
      And would you not do much to do her good?

Duplass. To do her good I would sustain some harm.

Contessa. What would you do?

Duplass. More I would than for myself I dare;
      Till necessity be served.

Contessa. Tonight come by and by to my chamber.

Duplass. Most insatiate and luxurious woman!
      I shall be forsworn;
      Put not another sin upon my head.

Contessa. Might not there be a charity in sin
      To save a sister's life?

Duplass. (Shaken at the threat.)
      Why do you speak so startlingly and rash?

Contessa. I speak no more than what my soul intends;
      And that is to enjoy thee for my love.

Duplass. How can you woo me so? I beseech you
      To curb your cruel father of his will.
      Speak to the duke; see if you can move him.

Contessa. If you come to me soon at night.

Duplass. If you will sign a pardon for Martine.

Contessa. I have not the power.

Duplass. Then with most out-stretch'd throat I'll tell
     the world aloud
What woman thou art!

Contessa. Who will believe you?
     My vouch against you, and my place in the state,
     Will so your accusation overweigh,
     That you shall stifle in your own report
     And smell of calumny.
     Say what you can, my false outweighs your true.

Duplass. How ill beseeming is it in thy sex
     To triumph, like an Amazonian trull,
     Upon their woes whom Fortune captivates!

Contessa. Redeem thy sister:
     Give thy sensual race the rein.

Duplass. I must not break my faith.

Contessa. We will talk further;
     Tend me to-night two hours, I ask no more.

       *Contessa walks away. Nonplussed, Duplass
          returns to his seat.*

Martine. What did Contessa whisper in your ear?

Duplass. She bid me stand no more off,
     But give myself unto her sick desires.

Martine. Foh! one may smell in such a will most rank,
  Foul disproportion, thoughts unnatural;
  O deeper sin than bottomless conceit
  Can comprehend in still imagination!
  The image of a wicked heinous fault
  Lives in her eye; her wanton spirits look out
  At every joint and motive of her body;
  Do not let her tempt you again to bed,
  To the rank sweat of an enseamed bed,
  And lull you while she playeth on her back.
  O Duplass, yield not to her.

  Duplass stares glumly ahead. Contessa has
  returned to the table where Balthus, having
  made his way over to Arnaud, is speaking to
  him. She bends over one of Arnaud's
  shoulders and massages the other.

Balthus. She is virtuous, and too well given
  To dream on evil or to work thy downfall.

Contessa. Do not say what a paragon she is.

Balthus. By noting of the lady I have mark'd
  That in her eye there hath appear'd a fire
  To burn the errors that your lordship holds
  Against her.

Contessa. So turns she every man the wrong side out.
  O, what authority and show of truth
  Can cunning sin cover itself withal!

Balthus. Her looks do argue her replete with modesty.

Arnaud. Yet see, Lord Balthus,
  When these so noble benefits shall prove

Not well disposed, the mind growing once corrupt,
They turn to vicious forms.

Balthus. Call me a fool;
Trust not my reading nor my observations;
Trust not my age, my reverence, nor calling,
If this sweet lady lie not guiltless here
Under some biting error.

Arnaud. What! Lack I credit?

Contessa. Come, gentlemen, we sit too long on trifles.
She something spoke in choler, ill, and hasty;
Her heart's her mouth;
What her breast forges, that her tongue must vent;
Then go about it: put her to choler straight:
Being once chafed, she cannot
Be rein'd again to temperance; then she speaks
What's in her heart; and that is there which looks
With us to break her neck.

Arnaud. Let her perceive how ill we brook her treason,
And what offence it is to flout our grace.
Call her to present trial; if she may
Find mercy in the law, 'tis hers; if none,
Let her not seek 't of us.

> *Balthus returns to the dais. Lacoste and*
> *Duplass speak confidentially.*

Duplass. Mark, how they whisper;
High-stomached are they both, and full of ire.

Lacoste. Now, by heaven, Duplass, I do perceive
An unnaturalness between the child
And the parent.

Duplass. Then you perceive the body of our land;
      How foul it is; what rank diseases grow
      And with what danger, near the heart of it.

Lacoste. This tyrant Arnaud was once thought honest.

Duplass. And if his wisdom be misled in this,
      The practice of it lives in Contessa,
      Whose spirits toil in frame of villainies.
      I fear Lord Balthus' wits begin t'unsettle.

Lacoste. Thus do the hopes we have in him touch
      ground.

> *Arnaud pushes back his chair and stands,
> getting everyone's attention.*

Arnaud. Thou, robed man of justice, take thy place.

Balthus. It's fit the royal session do proceed;
      And that, without delay, the arguments
      Be now produced and heard.

> *All arrange their chairs and sit, except Arnaud.*

Arnaud. Arraign her straight.

Lacoste. *(Standing.)* We do beseech your lordship,
      That, in this case of justice, the accusers,
      Be what they will, may stand forth face to face,
      And freely urge against us
      The examinations, proofs, confessions
      Of diverse witnesses, brought *viva voce.*

Balthus. It shall be done, my learned counsel.

Lacoste. Now depose her in the justice of her cause.

Arnaud and Lacoste sit. Martine stands.

Balthus. What is thy name? and wherefore comest thou
      hither?
   Against whom comest thou? and what's thy
      quarrel?

Martine. Lady Martine, wife of Pascal de Luc,
   The late deceased son of Duke Arnaud;
   Deprived of honor and inheritance,
   My suit is now to repossess my husband's lands,
   Seized on by Duke Arnaud,
   Which he in justice cannot well deny.

Balthus. Lady Martine, I do in justice charge thee,
   On thy soul's peril and thy body's torture,
   That you will answer all things faithfully,
   And forswear not thyself.

Martine. I will tell truth; by grace itself I swear.

Balthus directs Martine to take her seat.

Balthus. Proceed, Duke. Read the indictment.

Lacoste. (Correcting Balthus.) First ask his name and
      orderly proceed
   To swear him in the justice of his cause.

Balthus. Say who thou art and wherefore comest thou
      hither;
   Against whom comest thou? and what's thy
      quarrel?

Arnaud. (Standing.) I am Arnaud, the duke of all this
      realm;
   And I charge the Lady Martine de Luc

Of most vile outrageous crimes
Committed by her person against the state.

Balthus. Do you, sir,
Swear by the duty that you owe to God
To keep the oath that we administer?

Arnaud. *(Raising his hand.)* I here take my oath before
this assembly,
And let heaven be the record of my speech.

Duplass. And God forbid his grace should be forsworn.

Arnaud. Pray you, tread softly.

Martine. His oaths and laws will prove an idle scorn.

Lacoste puts a hand on Martine's arm.

Balthus. *(To Lacoste.)* By your leave, sir, it fits we thus
proceed.
(To Arnaud.)
Now, Duke, read the indictment.

*Contessa slides a piece of paper over to Arnaud.
He picks it up and reads.*

Arnaud. <u>Lady Martine, thou art a traitor,</u>
<u>Conspirant 'gainst our high-illustrious self,</u>
<u>And art attaint with faults and perjury,</u>
<u>Contrary to the faith and allegiance</u>
<u>Of a true subject. Thou art here accused</u>
<u>And arraigned of high treason.</u>
(Waving the paper.)
Such is thy audacious wickedness.

Martine. (Disbelieving.) Please you to repeat. What is
    my offence?

Arnaud. Manifest treason!

Martine. A lie, an odious, damned, wicked lie:
    In thy foul throat thou liest!

Duplass. Thou wrong'st a gentle lady, who is as far
    From thy report as thou from honor.

Arnaud. Sirrah, be gone, or talk not, I advise you.
    I would you had some cause to prattle for yourself.

Martine. Thou art a villain to impeach me thus.
    If thou deny'st it twenty times, thou liest;
    And I will turn thy falsehood to thy heart,
    Where it was forged.

Lacoste tries again to keep Martine calm.

Arnaud. I'll prove mine honor and my honesty
    Against thee presently.
    Touching our person seek we no revenge:
    But we our kingdom's safety must so tender,
    That to her laws we do deliver you.
    We will prosecute by good advice.

Martine. Have I lived thus long, never yet branded
    With suspicion, and am thus rewarded?
      (To Balthus.)
    I beseech your grace that I may know
    The worst that may befall me in this case.

Balthus. The justice and the truth o' th' question carries
    The due of the verdict with it;
    I'll see your trial first, and the evidence.

For we will hear, note, and believe in heart
That what you speak is in your conscience washed
As pure as sin with baptism.

Arnaud. Because of all those things you have done of
      late,
Our further pleasure is
That therefore a writ be sued against you;
To forfeit all your goods and lands, and to be
Out of our protection.

Martine. Alas, my lord, what cause
Hath my behavior given to your displeasure,
That thus you should proceed to put me off,
And take your good grace from me?
The purest spring is not so free from mud
As I am clear from treason; if, in the course
And process of this time, you can report,
And prove it too, against mine honor aught,
Turn me away; and let the foul'st contempt
Shut door upon me, and so give me up
To the sharp'st kind of justice.

Arnaud. Well hast thou lesson'd us. This shall we do.
      (To Balthus.)
Pleaseth his grace to answer them directly
How far forth he doth like the articles.

Balthus. (Sputters.) Extraordinary. I must think.
      (Pause.)
We will consider of this further.

Arnaud. Take your time, sir. Meanwhile, Lady
      Martine,
I arrest thee on capital treason.

Lacoste. (Leaping to his feet.)
>This must not be! Chief Justice Balthus,
>Wherefore? O, answer me, sir!

Martine. Now help, ye choice spirits that admonish me:
>Appear and aid me.

Arnaud. Hear her!
>This supernatural soliciting cannot be good;
>She is a naughty person, lewdly bent,
>Dealing with witches and conjurers,
>Raising up wicked spirits from underground;
>A practiser of arts inhibited and out of warrant.

Martine. This is mere madness; sure, the man is mad.
>'Tis such stuff as madmen tongue and brain not.

Arnaud. She does abuse our ears; to prison with her!
>Chief Justice Balthus, I demand that you
>Arrest her to the answer of the law;
>And God acquit her of her practices!

*Lacoste. (Approaching Balthus, his hands
>outstretched.)*
>Where are the evidence that do accuse her?
>What lawful quest have given their verdict up,
>Before she be imprison'd?
>>*(Pausing while he awaits a response.)*
>Lord Balthus, I sent your grace
>The parcels and particulars of our griefs,
>The which hath been with scorn shoved from the
>>court
>With our most right and just desires. Wherefore?
>If it please your honor, answer me, sir!

Martine. My lord, do you suffer me to be imprison'd?

Balthus. (Barely collecting himself.)
    Duke Arnaud, what reason have you for't?

Arnaud. Sir, we have thought it good
    From our person she should be confined,
    Lest that witchcraft be left her to perform.
    Take her away; to prison with her till fit time
    Of law and course of direct session
    Call her to answer.

Lacoste. My lord, I desire you do her right and justice;
    And bestow your pity on her, having here
    No judge indifferent besides yourself;
    I do beseech you,
    Bear with her weakness, which I think proceeds
    From prolonged sorrow, and no grounded malice;
    From the remembrance of her husband's death,
    Whose loss hath pierced her deep and scarr'd her
        heart;
    And rather comfort her distressed plight
    Than prosecute for these contempts.
    Shall we have justice? What says Lord Balthus?

Balthus. (Flustered.) Fear not, Lacoste; I shall give you
    justice.

Arnaud. Ay, as thou urgest justice, be assured
    Thou shalt have justice, more than thou desirest.
    Take her away.

Martine. O, break, my heart! poor bankrupt, break at
    once!

Curtain.

END OF ACT I.

ACT II

Scene 1

*The hearing room. Another day. Balthus,
Arnaud, and Contessa sit at their places,
Duplass and Lacoste at theirs. Martine
enters and sits between them.*

Duplass. How wert thou handled, being prisoner?

Martine. With scoffs and scorns and contumelious
      taunts;
    All the whole time I was my chamber's prisoner.

Duplass. I grieve to hear what torments you endured;
    But we will be revenged sufficiently.
    Be comforted, dear sister.

Martine. Comfort is too far for me to expect.
    Boiling choler chokes
    The hollow passage of my poison'd voice,
    By sight of these my baleful enemies.

Lacoste. Let's be calm; thou art in a parlous state.

Martine. Is not my sorrow deep, having no bottom?
    Then be my passions bottomless with them.

Arnaud clears his throat and stands.

Lacoste. Be calm, be calm, now. Listen but speak not.

Contessa lightly touches Arnaud's wrist and
he speaks.

Arnaud. Lord Balthus, by your leave we shall begin.

Balthus. All art sworn. Proceed.

Contessa slides some papers to Arnaud.

Arnaud. Lady Martine de Luc, we undertake
To show how much thou art degenerate.

Martine. Do not think so; you shall not find it so:
And God forgive them that so much have sway'd
Your highness' fair thoughts away from me.
'Tis such as you,
    (To Contessa.)
That creep like shadows by him and do sigh
At each his needless heavings;
You that are thus so tender o'er his follies,
Will never do him good.

Arnaud. Upon thy certainty and confidence
What darest thou venture?

Martine. With vilest torture let my life be ended.

Arnaud. Then for the truth and plainness of the case,
If it please your honor, view these letters.

Arnaud takes the letters to Balthus and waits
while Balthus looks them over.

Balthus. What, worse and worse!

Arnaud takes back the letters and selects one
of them.

Balthus. There are some shrewd contents in yond
　　　papers.

Arnaud. What's here? The sharp thorny points
　　　Of my alleged reasons. I will read it.
　　　　　(Reads first letter.)
　　　Dear husband, Your father's wrath, should he take
　　　me in his dominion, would be cruel to me. You
　　　have many opportunities to cut him off. If your will
　　　want not, time and place will be fruitfully offered.
　　　Let our reciprocal vows be remembered.
　　　Yet more!

　　　*With a glance at Contessa, he makes a show of
　　　taking a second letter and reads it aloud.*

Arnaud. Dearest Husband, I begin to find an idle
　　　bondage in the oppression of aged tyranny; who
　　　sways, not as it hath power, but as it is suffered.
　　　This policy and reverence for age keeps our fortunes
　　　from us. If your father would sleep till I waked him,
　　　you should enjoy his revenue for ever. If thou fear
　　　to strike and to make me certain that it is done,
　　　thou art to me disloyal. Thy true and loyal wife,
　　　Martine.
　　　　　(Shaking the letters in the air.)
　　　There is much more, much worse!

Martine. Forgeries!

　　　*After another glance at Contessa, who nods
　　　almost imperceptibly, Arnaud makes a show
　　　of taking a third letter. He reads it aloud.*

Arnaud. Our plot is a good plot, as ever was laid. Thy
　　　oath remember, thou hast sworn to do't. 'Tis but a
　　　blow, which never shall be known. Thou canst not

<u>do a thing in the world so soon to yield thee so
much profit. Let not conscience thy bosom enslave
too nicely; but be a soldier to thy purpose. She that
remains loyal to her vow, Thy wife.</u>
    (Waving the letters in the air.)
With her husband to plot against my life!
O undistinguish'd space of woman's will!
See thyself, devil! Proper deformity
Shows not in the fiend so horrid as in woman.

Lacoste. But I have not seen these letters.
Lord Balthus, again I do protest.

Arnaud. Why, what need we commune with you of this,
But rather follow our forceful instigation?
Our prerogative calls not your counsels.

    *Arnaud lays all the letters in front of Lacoste,
    who quickly examines them and passes them
    to Martine; she looks at them.*

Duplass. (While Martine reads.)
The Lady Martine hath been falsely accused!
She is wronged, she is slandered, she is undone.

Martine. What excellent falsehood!
These letters shall not henceforth trouble me.
Here is a coil with protestation!

    Martine tears the letters.

Arnaud. Why, how now!
What see you in those papers that you lose
So much complexion? Why, what read you there
That hath so cowarded and chased your blood
Out of appearance?

Lacoste. (Putting a hand on Martine's shoulder.)
    Seal up the mouth of outrage for a while,
    Till we can clear these ambiguities,
    And then will I be general of your woes,
    And lead you even to death: meantime forbear.

Martine. Will I stop mine ears against this calumny,
    And fawn on him with base humility?
    Let me speak myself, Monsieur Lacoste.
    I am no child; no babe.

Lacoste. Put not your worthy rage into your tongue:
    This nor hurts him nor profits you a jot;
    Forbear it therefore; and let your reason
    With your choler question what 'tis you go about.
    One time will owe another.

Martine. No, I will speak.

Lacoste. You lend no ear unto my purposes;
    I beseech you, let me answer the inter'gatories.

Martine. I pray thee, cease thy counsel.

Lacoste. The silence of pure innocence
    May persuade when speaking fails.

Martine. My tongue will tell the anger of my heart—

Lacoste. Truly I do fear it.

Martine. —Or else my heart concealing it will break.

Lacoste. Thou hast amazed me:
    I thought thy disposition better temper'd.

Martine. (To Arnaud, pointing at the shredded letters.)
Counterfeit, Duke Arnaud, I assure you.

Arnaud. This is not counterfeit.

Martine. I say I never did invent these letters;
This is a man's invention and his hand.
            (Wielding a pen in her hand.)
Bring me to the test: let proof speak.

            *Arnaud sees how this challenge damages his
            credibility, but just ignores it and asserts his
            own certainty.*

Arnaud. We need not; there is too great
Testimony in your complexion.

Martine. Ha! So! False forgeries!
These words hereafter thy tormentors be!

Arnaud. (With a finality to settle the issue.)
We are contented; every one
Of these letters are written in her hand.

Lacoste. To vouch this, Duke Arnaud, is no proof!

Martine. Through the false passage of thy throat, thou
      liest.
Recant! Unsay it now! Recant!

Arnaud. You may as well go stand upon the beach
And bid the main flood bate his usual height;
You may as well do anything most hard.

            Arnaud sits.

Martine. What lies I have heard! Giant-rude invention!
 I am sick of this false world.
　(Aside.)
 My resolution's placed. Boldness be my friend!
 Arm me, audacity, from head to foot!
 I must forget to be a woman: change
 Fear and niceness into a waggish courage;
 Throw away respect,
 Tradition, form, and ceremonious duty;
 And seek to thrive by that which has undone me.
　(To Balthus.)
 Lord Chief Justice, may I speak further?

Balthus. Speak thy mind, Lady Martine.

Arnaud. Let not her smoothing words bewitch your
　　heart;
 In her simple show she harbors treason.

Martine. Your grace, I would I could
 Quit all offences I am charged withal.
 Since what I am to say must be but that
 Which contradicts my accusation, and
 The testimony on my part no other
 But what comes from myself, it shall scarce boot me
 To say "not guilty": mine integrity
 Being counted falsehood, shall, as I express it,
 Be so received. Yet my tongue shall utter all;
 For me, I am the mistress of my fate.

Arnaud. There is no terror, Lady, in your threats;
 I fear nothing what can be said against me,
 For I am arm'd so strong in honesty
 That they pass by me as the idle wind.
 But she will speak most bitterly and strange.

Martine. Most strange, but yet most truly, will I speak:
    That the duke is forsworn; is it not strange?
    That the duke is adulterous, an hypocrite;
    Is it not strange? 'Tis not impossible
    But one, the wicked'st caitiff on the ground,
    May seem as grave, as just, as absolute
    As Duke Arnaud; even so may the duke
    In all his dressings, characts, titles, forms,
    Be an arch-villain; believe it, my lord,
    If he be less, he's nothing; but he's more,
    Had I more name for badness.

Balthus. How understand we that?

Martine. To speak so indirectly I am loath:
    I would say the truth: to accuse him so,
    That is your part.

Balthus. Be ruled by me.
    What mean you in this which you accuse him?

Martine. He would have forc'd my honor and my love;
    He hath commanded me to go to bed,
    And fit my consent to his sharp appetite,
    By yielding up my body to his will.

Arnaud. Infinite and endless liar! Wicked creature!
    Have you no modesty, no touch of bashfulness?
    Are you not ashamed with this clamorous outrage?

Martine. As I have told you, my Lord Chief Justice,
    The duke swore consent to my succession;
    But when I would not yield to be his whore,
    He broke his oath and resolution like
    A twist of rotten silk, and told me plain
    I must lay down the treasures of my body
    Or I shall not have my husband's lands.

Arnaud. I'll have your head for this your traitor's
    speech!

Martine. I told him plain, I had rather lie in prison
    Than give up my body to such uncleanness,
    For by that loss I would not purchase them.

Arnaud. Have done! for shame, if not for charity.

Martine. Urge neither charity nor shame to me:
    Uncharitably with me have you dealt,
    And shamefully by you my hopes are butcher'd.
    My charity is outrage, life my shame.
        (To Balthus.)
    Ay, that incestuous, that adulterous
    Beast would not, but by gift of my body
    To his concupiscible intemperate lust,
    Let me have what is mine.

Arnaud. *(Jumping up.)* Perjury, perjury, in the high'st
        degree!
    How like a swine she lies!
    Madam, there's no room for faith, truth,
    Nor honesty in this bosom of thine.

Martine. Sir, in this sin you are as deep as I.

Arnaud. Whose tongue soe'er speaks false
    Not truly speaks; who speaks not truly, lies!

Martine. Arnaud, thou art the nonpareil of this.
    Thou bloody, bawdy villain! Remorseless,
    Treacherous, lecherous, kindless villain!

Arnaud. As you are past all shame, so past all truth.

Martine. Swelling passion chokes my pleading tongue.
    (Aside.)
    Back foolish tears, back to your native spring.

Arnaud. Strike me the counterfeit matron; impudent
    Strumpet! She'll do any thing for gold;
    Lewd, pestiferous, and dissentious;
    Lascivious, wanton, more than well beseems
    A woman of her degree—a fornicatress.

Martine. Talk thy tongue weary; I have heard I am
    A wanton fornicatress; and mine ear
    Therein false struck, can take no greater wound.
    These words of yours draw life-blood from my
        heart;
    My spirit can no longer bear these harms;
    Your honor, the duke hath so bewhored me,
    Thrown such despite and heavy terms upon me,
    As true hearts cannot bear.

Arnaud. As for your spiteful false accusations,
    Prove them, and I lie open to the law.

Martine. All know his own opinion is his law.

Balthus. I pray you, tell me what you mean by that.

Arnaud. If I may be heard, I would crave a word!

Martine. He would say untruths; and be ever double
    Both in his words and meaning. As I told thee,
    He professes not keeping of oaths; he will lie,
    Sir, with such volubility that you would
    Think truth were a fool.

Arnaud. Dear my lord, hear me! I crave the law!
    Justice, my lord, against that woman there!

That hath abused and dishonour'd me
Even in the strength and height of injury!

Duplass. *(Aside.)* Meantime, the duke's cheeks look
     pale with fear,
As witnessing the truth on our side.

Arnaud. Beyond imagination is the wrong
     That she this day hath shameless thrown on me.
Will I have mine honor soil'd
With the attainder of her slanderous lips?
Taunted with such full license as malice
Has power to utter?
Madam, you do me wrong; but my fair name
To dark dishonor's use thou shalt not have.

Martine. *Thy* fair name?! *I* am wronged; *I* am undone;
I am disgraced, impeach'd and baffled here,
Pierced to the soul with slander's venom'd spear.

Arnaud. By all my hopes, most falsely doth she lie.

Balthus. Speak truth, lady: hath some one set you on?
Say by whose advice thou camest here to complain.

Martine. Herein I did have use of *your* advice,
Lord Balthus; *you* did bid me name my griefs.

Balthus. Your sense pursues not mine; either you are
     ignorant,
Or seem so craftily, and that's not good.

Arnaud. She has undone a man of threescore years,
That thought to fill his grave in quiet.

Martine. Your wrong doth equal mine.
Thereby we stand opposed by such means

As you yourself have forged against me
By unkind usage, dangerous countenance,
And violation of all faith and troth.

Arnaud. Lord Balthus, I beseech thee, let me have way
To dispense all the rigor of the law.

Balthus. We must be wise and circumspect;
The sessions shall proceed lawfully.

Arnaud. Good my lord, give me the scope of justice.

Lacoste. Your honor, if his will pass, we shall both
Find the duke judge and juror. I ask again,
Is this proceeding just and honorable?

Balthus. Monsieur Lacoste, what would you have me
do?

Lacoste. My Lord Chief Justice, truth loves open
dealing;
Let reason serve to make the truth appear
Where it seems hid, and hide the false seems true.

Arnaud. The truth appears so naked on my side
That any purblind eye may find it out.

Lacoste. Please your grace, give me leave to show
That the duke is most unmeet of any man
To accuse this worthy woman.

Balthus. I will hear it all. Proceed, Counsellor.

Lacoste. First, her integrity
Stands without blemish. Next, it imports no reason
That with such vehemency the duke hath
Slandered, scarred, and dishonored her

With public accusation and unmitigated rancor.
To justify this worthy noblewoman,
So vulgarly and personally accused,
The duke shall you hear disproved to his eyes,
Till he himself confess it.

*Lacoste comes from behind the table to
face Arnaud.*

Lacoste. Duke Arnaud, Lady Martine doth claim
That you importuned her by vehement suit
To make room for you in her late husband's bed,
To partake in shameful sport, sinful loving,
And wicked deeds. Is not this true?

Arnaud. No, it is false.

Lacoste. Meant you to enjoy her?

Arnaud. Never.

Lacoste. Have you importuned her by any means?

Arnaud. None. She's a measureless liar.

Lacoste. Would you not have pick'd the lock and taken
The treasure of her honor?

Arnaud. Not I, I assure thee.

Lacoste. Hast a thing within thee called conscience?
Thou art religious; confess the truth.

Arnaud. Monsieur Lacoste, I took an oath;
When I break that oath, let me turn monster.
I shall maintain what I have said is true.
I cared not for her, and I claimed her not.

She knew her distance and did angle for me,
Madding my eagerness with her cunning.
She knows the heat of a luxurious bed.

Duplass. You never spoke what did become you less
than this.
Thou dost belie her, and thou art a devil.

*Arnaud gives Duplass a menacing look, but
is visibly anxious and glances at Contessa,
who does not acknowledge him.*

Arnaud. I have spoke the truth.

Lacoste. You something seem unsettled,
As if you held a brow of much distraction:
Are you moved, my lord?

Arnaud. No, in good earnest.

Lacoste. *(Suddenly changing tactic.)*
Seek you to seize and gripe into your hands
The royalties and rights of Lady Martine?

Arnaud. What if I do?

Lacoste. By what authority?

Arnaud. The sovereign power I have of her.

Lacoste. You have too lavishly wrested authority,
If you deny Lady Martine her rights.

Arnaud. The laws are mine, not thine.
Who can arraign me for't?

Lacoste. This court.

Arnaud. I must not believe you. You mistake, sir.

Lacoste. I do not mistake:
But thou mistakest me much to think I do.

Arnaud. Think what you will, we seize into our hands
Her plate, her goods, her money, and her lands.

Lacoste. If we have law, thou shall repent this rape.

Arnaud. Rape, call you it, Monsieur, to seize my own?

Lacoste. Duke, you allege, on your authority,
Many sharp reasons to defeat the law.
More than so, you are unjust.

Arnaud. Meanwhile I am possess'd of that is mine.

Lacoste. These things indeed you have articulate.
(Pausing, then shifting tactic again.)
But, my lord, this doth prompt me to inquire:
Are you acquainted with the difference
That holds the present question in the court?

Arnaud. I was advised by my learned counsel.

Lacoste. Alack, sir, you do usurp authority
If you deny Lady Martine her rights.
And unless my study and books be false,
The argument you hold is wrong in you;
Your reasons are too shallow and too quick,
For stubbornly you do repugn the truth
About a certain question. Resolve me this:
Lady Martine was the wife of Pascal;
Doth not she live, and is not Pascal dead?
Is not his heir a well-deserving wife?
Take her rights away, and take from Time

His charters and his customary rights;
Let not tomorrow then ensue today;
Be not thyself; for how art thou a duke
But by fair sequence and succession?
Now, if you do wrongfully seize her rights,
And call in the letters patent that she hath,
You pluck a thousand dangers on your head,
You lose a thousand well-disposed hearts,
And prick our tender patience to those thoughts
Which honor and allegiance cannot think.

Arnaud. He that holds the dukedom holds the law.

Lacoste. You speak, Duke Arnaud, now you know not
    what.
    (To Balthus.)
My lord, you have heard from Lady Martine
That he importuned her to vile offence,
And would have forc'd her honor and her love;
That he broke his oath and told her
She must yield up her body to his will,
Or she shall not have her husband's lands.
Further I say, and further will maintain,
That, to obtain his lust, Lady Martine
Hath been falsely, personally, accused
And arraigned of high treason,
To put the strong law on her, unless she
Do submit herself to this lustful lord.

    Pause; Balthus is attentive but reluctant
        to speak.

Balthus. Indeed.

Lacoste. My lord, you have heard the duke confess that,
    By his authority, he seizes into his hands
    Her plate, her goods, her money, and her lands;

And he declares the laws are his, not ours.
Moreover, he would be both the plaintiff
And the judge of his own cause. Your honor,
The duke cannot deny the course of law;
Or bid the law make court'sy to his will;
What will ensue hereof, there's none can tell.
What shall we say to this in law, my lord?
    (Long pause for Balthus to answer.)
Chief Justice Balthus? Dost thou attend me?

Balthus. Most heedfully.

Lacoste. Then what sayest thou to this in law?

Balthus. What you have said, sir, I will consider.

Lacoste. You must consider! May't please your
      highness
To resolve us now. Even on the instant!

Arnaud. You heard the justice say himself:
    He must needs consider further.

Lacoste. (To Balthus.) No more evasion, sir; delay it
    not.

Arnaud. O ye gods! Monsieur Lacoste, seest thou not?
    The laws of the land are at my commandment!

Lacoste. But 'tis not so, Duke Arnaud;
    You are deceived; 'tis not so;
    Lord Chief Justice, as thou know'st well—

Balthus. Yes, yes: "most strict statutes,
    Needful bits and curbs" et cetera.

Lacoste. Chief Justice, sir, be pleased to tell the duke
          That he his high authority hath abused:
          It is enacted: no power in the land
          Can alter a decree established,
          Or frame the law unto his will.

Arnaud. There naught hath pass'd but even with due
          course.

Lacoste. Your honor, he hath rush'd aside the law;
          What make you of this?
              (Pausing for a reply.)
          He must not rend his subjects from the laws,
          And stick them in his will. What say you, sir?

Balthus. Good master Lacoste, it is well objected.

Lacoste. "Well objected?" Is that all?
          If that be right which the duke says is right,
          There is no wrong, but every thing is right.

Balthus. I will not bandy with thee word for word.
          This candle burns not clear.

Lacoste. What plain proceeding is more plain than
          this?
              (Pausing for reply.)
          Doth it not shake our peace and safety
          To see our most dreadful laws so loosely slighted?
              *(Pausing for reply while Balthus stares at his
              desk.)*
          To such proceeding
          Who ever but his approbation added,
          Though not his prime consent, he did not flow
          From honorable sources.
              (Pausing for reaction.)
          Ye gods, it doth amaze me

A man of such feeble learning should
So get the office of a chief justice.

Balthus. Do you call me fool?
Upon my power I may dismiss this court!

Lacoste. You may, sir, and give Duke Arnaud leave
To pluck down justice from your awful bench,
To trip the course of law and blunt the sword
That guards the peace and safety of the land.
But in the name of justice, Lord Balthus,
You have the power to be bold and resolute,
To enforce the laws, and seal the duke's lips.

Balthus. Was ever a chief justice thus overborne,
Confronted thus, and, used in such contempt?
Counsellor Lacoste, I have too long borne
Your blunt upbraidings and your bitter scoffs:
I'll not be made a soft and dull-eyed fool,
To shake the head, relent, and sigh, and yield.

Duplass. You already have, Lord Balthus.
You have done already.

Lacoste. Chief Justice, to your notorious shame,
We will have law in this case.

Balthus. Speak on, sir, I dare your worst objections.

Lacoste. If you deny us, fie upon your law!
There is no force in the decrees of the land.
We stand for judgment: answer, shall we have it?
Or will you deny us?

Balthus. (Whispering across his desk to Lacoste.)
Monsieur Lacoste, softly, hear me what I say:

I do it not in evil disposition,
But from the duke himself by special charge.

Lacoste. Then we do refuse you for our judge.

Balthus. (Beleaguered, to Lacoste.)
    Patience, Counsellor. The book of law
    You shall yourself read after your own sense.
        (To Martine.)
    Madam, we will consider of your suit,
    And come some other time to know our mind.
        (To All.)
    We adjourn this court till
    A verdict is determined.

Blackout.

ACT II

Scene 2

Immediately after the adjournment. In the duke's official meeting chamber. Contessa, Arnaud, and Balthus deliberate around his desk.

Contessa. (To Balthus.) I am right glad that she's so
    out of hope.
    Do not, for one repulse, forego the purpose
    That you resolved to effect.

Balthus. Duke Arnaud, my duty cannot suffer
    T' obey in all your daughter's hard commands.

Arnaud. I do beseech your grace to pardon her;
    Her duty cannot be silent.

Balthus. In the administration of the law,
    Her highness pleases to forget my place,
    The majesty and power of law and justice,
    And strikes me in my very seat of judgment.

Arnaud. Be you contented. You have served me well.

Contessa. We have found her guilty of high treason.

Balthus. (After a dumbfounded pause.)
    As for proof, what evidence?

Contessa. She was charged with nothing but what was
    true.

Balthus. As it is said, to vouch this is no proof.
    Many other evidences proclaim her
    With all certainty to be innocent.

Contessa. Lady Martine is obstinate,
    Stubborn to justice, apt to accuse it,
    And disdainful to be tried by't; she defies
    Those whose great power must try her.

Balthus. The reasons you allege do more conduce
    To the hot passion of distemper'd blood
    Than to make up a free determination
    'Twixt right and wrong.

Contessa. My lord, you have enough: be you content;
    We beg the law, the law, upon her head.

        Contessa stares severely at Arnaud until
              he speaks.

Arnaud. She hath betrayed me and shall die the death.

Balthus. (Alarmed.) Condemn'd to die? A heavy
        sentence, Duke,
    And all unlook'd for from your lordship's mouth.

Arnaud. I hope we shall see an end of her.

Contessa. The remedy indeed to do us good
    Is to let forth her foul-defiled blood.
    Urge the necessity of the verdict.

Balthus. In such haste? Why so? Pray be counsell'd:
    A night is but small breath and little pause
    To answer matters of this consequence.

Arnaud. (Aside to Contessa.) But yet we want a color
       for her death:
   'Tis meet she be condemned by course of law.
   And yet we have but trivial argument.

Contessa. We need no more, my lord.
   Chief Justice Balthus, proceed to judgment.

Balthus. I beseech your highness, forbear this talk;
   Hear me with patience but to speak a word:
   Lady Martine, dying, shall be lamented
   And excused of every hearer;
   Her virtues will plead like angels against
   The deep damnation of her taking-off.

Arnaud. I have considered so much.

Balthus. O, let us yet be merciful.

Contessa. Nothing emboldens sin so much as mercy;
   Pardon is still the nurse of second woe.

Arnaud. (His voice full of doubt.) One sin, I know,
       another doth provoke.

Contessa. If thou do pardon, whosoever pray,
   More sins for this forgiveness prosper may.

Arnaud. (To Contessa.) Yet have I my misgiving still.

Contessa. I could be well moved, if I were as you:
   But I am constant as the northern star.
   The tender love I bear your grace, makes me
   Most forward to doom the offender;
   I say she has deserved death.

Arnaud. I am perplex'd and overcome by doubt.

Contessa. Nay! My most worthy father, in your breast
  Doubt and suspect, alas, are placed too late.

Balthus. Modest doubt is call'd the beacon of the wise.

Contessa. In such a time it nothing becomes you;
  Quick consideration shall clear that doubt.

Arnaud. (Pleading.) Urge it no more, Contessa.

Contessa. (Jumping to her feet.) Infirm of purpose!
  O that you bore the mind that I do!
  Thou art a fool; she robs thee of thy name.

Arnaud. Tessa.

Contessa. My lord, pronounce sentence and subject her
  Unto the rigor of severest law.

Arnaud. Lord Balthus, may I pronounce a sentence?

Balthus. There is no such article within our law.

Contessa. Father, you may do your will;
  It is in your power to o'erthrow law.

Balthus. I beseech your grace: talk no more of this.

Contessa. Will you deny us now? Is't possible
  Our deserts to you can lack persuasion?

Balthus. This act so evilly born shall cool the hearts
  Of all the people: this will break out
  To all our sorrows, and ere long I doubt.

Contessa. Let us dispatch this with all speed.

Arnaud. By heaven, I will be satisfied;
　　No more talking on it; let it be done.

Balthus. Is it your will Lady Martine shall die?

Arnaud. (Irritated.) Why dost thou ask again?

Balthus. Lest we might be too rash: I have seen,
　　When, after execution, judgment hath
　　Repented o'er his doom.

Arnaud. I'll answer that. Your pains we thank you for.

　　　　*Arnaud seizes a pen and writes out a few
　　　　lines, then waves the paper at Contessa
　　　　and Balthus.*

Arnaud. For what I mean to do
　　See here in bloody lines I have set down;
　　And what is written shall be executed;
　　Firm and irrevocable is my doom;
　　And for this once my will shall stand for law.

Contessa. O just but severe law!

Balthus. (Overcome with despair.)
　　Our most dreadful laws so loosely slighted.
　　　　(Collecting himself.)
　　Alas, my lord, my honor is at pawn;
　　Is there no other way?

Contessa. There is no other way. Consent.

Balthus. (To Arnaud.) Must I?

Arnaud. Do you your office, or give up your place;
    And take heed, my lord;
    You are of our chamber, and our mind partakes
    Her private actions to your secrecy.

Blackout.

ACT II

Scene 3

Later that day. The formal hearing chamber.
Awaiting the verdict, Duplass paces anxiously;
Martine sits, preoccupied with her thoughts;
Lacoste sits, visibly anxious.

Duplass. Thou wouldst not think how ill all's here
     about
My heart. I'm wrapped in dismal thinkings.

Martine. Brother, make not thoughts your prison.

Duplass. I feel such sharp dissension in my breast;
     Such fierce alarums both of hope and fear,
     And I am sick with working of my thoughts;
     A chilling sweat o'er-runs my trembling joints.
          (Struggling to keep his composure.)
     I dare not say what I think, since I have found
     Myself in my incertain grounds to fail
     As often as I guess'd. But this I know:
     Arnaud is a soulless, wicked villain.

Lacoste. Hark you, Duplass; mark me:
     All three of them are desperate: their great guilt,
     Like poison given to work a great time after,
     Now 'gins to bite the spirits.

Duplass. *(Sitting beside Martine.)*
     Dear sister, I must tell you that it is
     Contessa who holds thee so under fortune.

Martine. I know this; this and much more.

Duplass. Of all things upon the earth
  She hates your person most, and is
  A villainous contriver against you.

Martine. All this I know. There is not one so young
  And so villainous this day living;
  My soul hates nothing more than she.

Duplass. She shut her ears against your suit.

Martine. Sure, you refused to answer her summons?

   Duplass hangs his head in shame.

Martine. You wronged yourself.
   (Pause while she retracts her judgment.)
  Brother, you thought to help me. Be absolved.
  And from my heart's love I do thank thee for it;
  A heavier task could not have been imposed.

Lacoste. Fear not; they will not prevail.

   Balthus, Arnaud, and Contessa enter and
   take their seats. Duplass' face loses hope;
   he groans softly.

Duplass. Lord Balthus' brow, like to a title-leaf,
  Foretells the nature of a tragic volume.

Balthus. (Without conviction, eyes on his desk.)
  Lady Martine de Luc, you have conspired
  Against the royal person; you stand attainted,
  Guilty of disloyalty and high treason;
  So, by the lawful power that I have,

Thou art condemn'd, and must endure our law.
I am sorry for thee.

Lacoste. Underhand corrupted foul injustice!
Outrageous! .By heaven! .May this be borne?

Duplass. You block, you stone, you worse than
senseless thing!
O you hard heart!
My thoughts are whirled like a potter's wheel;
I know not where I am, nor what I do.

Martine. Are these things spoken, or do I but dream?

Balthus. (Rising feebly from his seat.)
I beseech your lordship, give me leave to go.

Arnaud. Depart not so; come, come, and sit you down;
You shall not budge till we have done.

Balthus drops back into his chair.

Arnaud. Speak, Lord Balthus. Conclude, conclude.

Balthus. (Reluctantly, in a dull, rote voice.)
Because the intent and purpose of the law
Hath full relation to the penalty,
I, now the voice of the recorded law,
Pronounce a sentence; stand forth, Lady Martine.

Martine rises defiantly from her seat.

Balthus. God quit you in his mercy! Hear your
sentence.
Your guilt is great: look for no less than death.
Take her from hence to prison back again;
From thence unto the place of execution,

Where she shall be strangled on the gallows.
Lady Martine de Luc, prepare to die.

Balthus slumps in his seat, his moral being
collapsing.

Contessa. (Triumphantly.) So are all brought to the
correction of our law.

Lacoste. The guilt of conscience take thou for thy labor.

Martine. When will this fearful slumber have an end?

Arnaud. Lady, the law, thou see'st, hath judged thee.

Martine. Villain, thou know'st no law of God nor man.

Duplass. Would God that any in this noble presence
Were enough noble to be upright judge
Of this innocent lady.
Why should we be tender
To let an arrogant piece of flesh
Play judge and executioner, all himself?

Arnaud. Silence that fellow!

Lacoste. Duke Arnaud, we charge you
With making your will the scope of justice.

Arnaud. Stop close their mouths, let them not speak a
word.
Though the law hath slept, now 'tis awake.

Duplass. You have contrived to make the law a tyrant.

Arnaud. Judge, stop their mouths, let them not speak
to me!

Duplass. Think'st thou that conscience shall have dread
    to speak?
  O judgment! thou art fled to brutish beasts;
  The three of you have laid your heads together,
  And all to make away her guiltless life;
  I tell you, 'tis rigor and not law.

Arnaud. Good sir, be cur'd of this diseas'd opinion,
  And betimes; for 'tis most dangerous.
  This is the law, and this the lady's doom.
    (To Martine.)
  Here I disclaim all my paternal care,
  And as a stranger to my heart and me
  Hold thee for ever.

Lacoste. *(To Balthus.)* Have patience, sir! O, let it not
    be so!
  Herein you war against your reputation.
  Chief Justice Balthus, consider further
  The effects of sorrow for her husband,
  Her woeful self shut in a mourning house,
  Raining the tears of lamentation;
  The unhappy lady, in hot blood,
  Hath stepp'd into the law, which is past depth
  To those that, without heed, do plunge into't.

Balthus. Plead no more, Counsellor Lacoste;
  I am not partial to infringe our laws.

Lacoste. Good my Lord Chief Justice, I beseech you,
  Wrest once the law to your authority:
  Go to your bosom:
  Knock there, and ask your heart what it doth know;
  To do a great right, do a little wrong;
  Use your authority. Reverse your doom;
  And in your best consideration check
  This hideous rashness.

Arnaud. Lacoste, heed Lord Balthus: plead no more.
We cannot justify whom the law condemns.

*Duplass. (Getting up and then kneeling before
          Arnaud.)*
     Your lordship, on my knees
     I beg that you do change this purpose.

Arnaud. How now, how now, mad wag! No quips now,
     sir?

          Duplass retreats back to his seat.

Lacoste. Duke Arnaud, we appeal to your conscience:
     Before Martine came to your court, how she
     Was in your grace, how merited to be so.

Arnaud. Policy sits above conscience. I am deaf to
     pleading.

Lacoste. The very mercy of the law cries out!
     This most cruel usage something savors
     Of tyranny and will ignoble make you;
     Yea, scandalous to the world.

Arnaud. Dost call me "tyrant"? Again?
     The mercy that was quick in us but late
     By your own counsel is suppress'd and kill'd.

Lacoste. I pray, my lord, pardon me. Consider:
     No ceremony that to great ones 'longs,
     Not the king's crown, nor the deputed sword,
     The marshal's truncheon, nor the judge's robe,
     Become them with one half so good a grace
     As mercy does.
     Mercy is above the sceptred sway;
     Sweet mercy is nobility's true badge;

Wilt thou draw near the nature of our God?
Draw near him then in being merciful.
How shalt thou hope for mercy, rend'ring none?
How would you be, if He, which is the top
Of judgment, should but judge you as you are.
O, think on that, and mercy then will breathe
Within your lips like man new made.

> *Seeing that Arnaud is about to respond,*
> *Lacoste pauses. But Contessa touches*
> *Arnaud's wrist, they exchange glances,*
> *and Arnaud remains silent.*

Lacoste. My lord, if thou be'st, as thou art spoken,
The true decider of all injuries,
I do think that you might pardon her,
And neither heaven nor man grieve at the mercy,
If your noble grace would have some pity.

Arnaud. We may pity, though not pardon her;
The passed sentence may not be recall'd
But to our honor's great disparagement.

Lacoste. But might you do't, and do the world no
                wrong,
If so your heart were touch'd with some remorse?
For pity is the virtue of the law,
And none but tyrants use it cruelly.

Arnaud. (Angrily.) "Tyrant" yet once again?
She's sentenced; 'tis too late.

Lacoste. Your grace, is there no other way of mercy?

Arnaud. (Glancing once more at Contessa.)
None. By law she is condemned to die.

Duplass. Duke, yet show some pity.

Arnaud. I show it most of all when I show justice.

Lacoste. But mercy seasons justice.

Arnaud does not respond.

Lacoste. Duplass, here we see the monstrousness of
    man
    When he looks out in an ungrateful shape!
    And we all are men, Duke Arnaud,
    In our own natures frail, and capable
    Of our flesh—few are angels—out of which frailty
    And want of wisdom, you
    Have misdemeaned yourself, and not a little.

Arnaud. Take heed, be wary how you place your words.

Duplass. O, it is excellent to have a giant's strength;
    But it is tyrannous to use it like a giant.

Arnaud. Silence!

Duplass. I am sorry for thee, inhuman wretch,
    Uncapable of pity, void and empty
    From any dram of mercy.
    The devil take thy soul and damn thee black.

Arnaud. I'll note you in my book of memory,
    To scourge you for this.

Lacoste. My Lord Chief Justice, once more I pray you,
    Give bold way to your authority
    And labor still to save the lady's life.

Balthus. *(Aware of Arnaud and Contessa glaring at*
    him.)
A passed sentence may not be recalled.
    (Defeated, disgraced, and ashamed.)
My dear Lady Martine, think on thy sins,
And prepare thyself to death.

Arnaud. Speak and confess thee freely of thy offence.

Martine. Alas, what is my offence?
    (Pause.)
I wonder on't.
    (Pause.)
If I in act, consent, or sin of thought,
Be guilty of the accusations,
The law I bear no malice.
I do confess that I dared speak the truth,
And am richer than my base accusers,
That never knew what truth meant:
I would not buy
Your mercy at the price of one fair word.
What ignorant sin have I committed,
Which be of such mortal kind,
But dare accuse you of lust and rank thoughts,
Of deeds dishonorable and vile offence.
Thou art but a villain that filled
His vacancy with his voluptuousness,
Full surfeits, and the dryness of his bones.

Arnaud. Fell banning hag, enchantress, hold thy
    tongue!

Martine. First you bid me speak, now bid me hold my
    tongue;
I prithee, give me leave to curse awhile.

Arnaud. Curse, miscreant, when thou comest to the
  gallows.

> *Martine gathers herself with deep breaths*
> *and addresses her accusers.*

Martine. Sith there's no justice in earth or hell,
  I'll cry for vengeance at the gates of heaven.
  My curses light on thee
  So heavy as thou shalt not shake them off:
  The worm of conscience shall begnaw thy soul,
  Disturb your hours of rest with restless trances,
  Afflict you in your bed with bedrid groans.

Arnaud. Hide not thy poison with such sugar'd words.

Martine. All the infections that the sun sucks up
  From bogs, fens, flats on you fall and make you
  By inch-meal a disease!
  Of man and beast the infinite malady
  Crust you quite o'er that you may live
  Only in bone, that none may look on you!

Arnaud. Thou has spoke too much already; be silent!

Martine. No, no, I will not, having breath to cry:
  O, that my tongue were in the thunder's mouth!
  Then with a passion would I shake the world;
  I prophesy the fearful'st time to thee
  That ever wretched age hath look'd upon.

Arnaud. Silence! Rein thy tongue.

Martine. Live loathed and long,
  But in despair die under this black weight:
  May darkness and the gloomy shade of death
  Environ you, till mischief and despair

Drive you to break your neck or hang yourself!
And in that hope I throw mine eyes to heaven,
Scorning whate'er you can afflict me with.

Arnaud. Your curses and your blessings touch me alike.
    (Contessa lightly squeezes his hand.)
Get you hence to your death:
The taste whereof, God in his mercy give
You patience to endure, and true repentance
Of all your dear offences.

Martine. Live a thousand years,
I shall not find myself so apt to die.

Lacoste. Despair not, madam.

Martine. Who shall hinder me?
My heart, all mad with misery,
Beats in this hollow prison of my flesh.
    (Pause.)
Give sorrow leave awhile to tutor me
To this submission.
    (Pause.)
Now hear me speak my heart's deep languor:
Duke Arnaud, I thank thee, who hath taught
My frail mortality to know itself,
And to prepare this body to what I must;
Thus ready for death, I wait the sharpest blow.
My joy is death;
Death, at whose name I oft have been afeard
Because I wish'd this world's eternity;
Death, death; O amiable lovely death!
Thou odoriferous stench! sound rottenness!
Arise forth from the couch of lasting night,
And I will kiss thy detestable bones;
Misery's love, O, come to me!

Arnaud signals off-stage.

Arnaud. Take hence this traitor from our sight.

Martine. Lay not thy hands on me.
Desolate, desolate, will I hence and die;
I have given over, I will speak no more:
Do what you will. There is a world elsewhere.

Martine turns and begins walking away.

Arnaud. Ay, ay, away with her;
A little time will melt her.

Duplass. Her poor self walks, like contempt, alone.
Is it not pity, that we present here,
Were born to see so sad an hour as this?

Lacoste. Lest your sorrow should enlarge itself
To wrathful terms, let us depart, I pray you.

Exit Martine followed by Lacoste and Duplass.

Blackout.

ACT II

Scene 4

The next day. The cell where Martine is held. She sits alone, singing.

Martine. "Fear no more the heat o'th'sun,
  Nor the furious winter's rages,
  Thou thy worldly task has done,
  Home art gone and ta'en thy wages. . ."

Duplass enters. Martine is startled and embarrassed. He sits by her.

Martine. Duplass. Welcome, brother. I well could wish
  You had not found me here so musical.

Duplass tries throughout to keep up a cheerful façade.

Duplass. Better you were distract;
  So should thy thoughts be severed from thy griefs.
    (Pause.)
  There ran a rumor of some pardon or reprieve;
  My letters, praying on your side, were slighted off.
  The duke will not yield.

Martine. (Making a scoffing sound.)
  All's in vain. You wronged yourself to write.
    (Realizing she sounds ungrateful.)
  You thought to help me; and such thanks I give
  As one near death to those that wish her live.

Duplass. How hath you brooked imprisonment?

*Martine is preternaturally calm and
passive throughout.*

Martine. With patience, Duplass, as prisoners must.

Duplass. Their heavy hands hath beggar'd you for ever
    And bow'd you to the grave; do you find
    Your patience so predominant in your nature
    That you can let this go?

Martine. I feel within me
    A peace above all earthly dignities,
    A still and quiet conscience.

Duplass. Art not afeard?

Martine. I do arm myself
    To welcome the condition of the time;
    I am out of fear of death or death's hand.
    I do not set my life at a pin's fee;
    Tell me what blessings I have here alive,
    That I should fear to die.

Duplass. Thy brother's love; gentle friends.
    Thou'rt of all sorts enchantingly beloved,
    And, indeed, much in the heart of the world.

Martine. This world to me is like a lasting storm,
    Whirring me from my friends.
    The duke will have his will, and I must fall.

Duplass. I applaud your undaunted spirit.

Martine. Nor stony tower, nor walls of beaten brass,
    Not airless dungeon, nor strong links of iron,

Can be retentive to the strength of spirit:
But life being weary of these worldly bars
Never lacks power to dismiss itself.

Duplass. O, think not to prevent the time of life.
    (Looking around the cell.)
Give me the instrument to pick that bolt
And I'll direct thee how you shall escape.

Martine. Death. Death is the key to unbar these locks.

Duplass. Talk not of dying; death is a fearful thing:
    To die, and go we know not where;
    To lie in cold obstruction and to rot;
    This sensible warm motion to become
    A kneaded clod; and the delighted spirit
    To bathe in fiery floods, or to reside
    In thrilling region of thick-ribbed ice;
    To be imprison'd in the viewless winds,
    And blown with restless violence round about
    The pendent world; or to be worse than worst
    Of those that lawless and incertain thought
    Imagine howling: O, 'tis too horrible!
    The weariest and most loathed worldly life
    That age, ache, penury, and imprisonment
    Can lay on nature is a paradise
    To what we fear of death.

Martine. (Chuckling at his untimely dreariness.)
    I prithee, Duplass, have a better cheer!
    Death, as the Psalmist saith, is certain to all;
    Thoughts, the slaves of life, and life, time's fool,
    And time, that takes survey of all the world,
    Must have a stop.

Duplass. I prithee, lay aside life-harming heaviness;
    Be comforted.

Martine. No, I will not. All strange and terrible
　　　　Events are welcome, but comforts I despise;
　　　　I know my case is past hope, past help;
　　　　Have I not hideous death within my view?
　　　　　(Pause while she gazes into the distance.)
　　　　I feel now the future in the instant;
　　　　My grief stretches itself beyond the hour of death:
　　　　It engluts and swallows other sorrows;
　　　　The blood weeps from my heart when I do shape
　　　　In forms imaginary the unguided days
　　　　And rotten times that you shall look upon.

　　　　Duplass attempts to speak but chokes up.

Martine. Nay, good my brother, do not please sharp
　　　　　fate
　　　　To grace it with your sorrows:
　　　　Conquer fortune's spite;
　　　　Bid that welcome, which comes to punish us,
　　　　And we punish it, seeming to bear it lightly.

Duplass. Mad ire and wrathful fury make me weep;
　　　　Where are our friends and kindreds?

Martine. Afeard of the duke.
　　　　　(Comfortingly.)
　　　　Peace, brother.
　　　　Never more may I behold those comforts;
　　　　Never henceforth shall I joy again:
　　　　Things that are past are done with me;
　　　　The arbitrator of despairs,
　　　　Just death, doth dismiss me hence.
　　　　Now my soul's sad palace is become a prison:
　　　　Ah, would she break from hence, that this my body
　　　　Might in the ground be closed up in rest.

Duplass. Be thou still like thyself: let thy dauntless
      mind
    Still ride in triumph over all mischance.
    I honor thee, and will do till I die.
    (Weeping.)
    Dear Martine, I swear to thee,
    Vengeance is in my heart; blood and revenge
    Are hammering in my head; I'll venge thy death,
    Even by God, I swear to thee I will!
    Torture with grievous lingering death
    Were not revenge sufficient for me.

Martine. Duplass, think on revenge, and cease to weep.

    Martine takes his hand in hers, and uses
    a kerchief with her other hand.

Martine. Come, leave your tears:
    Let me wipe off this honorable dew
    That silverly doth progress on thy cheeks;
    A brief farewell.

Duplass. O, must I leave you? Must I needs forgo
    So good, so noble, and so true a sister?

Martine. I have told my last hour. Let us embrace.
    And whether we shall meet again, I know not:
    Therefore, our everlasting farewell take.

Duplass. Withhold thy speed, dreadful occasion.

    They embrace. He does not want to
    break off.

Martine. Even now be gone.

*Duplass finally breaks from the embrace
and hastily exits in tears. Martine sits
again, settles herself, and resumes her
singing.*

Martine. "Thou thy worldly task has done,
            Home art gone and ta'en thy wages:
            Golden lads and girls all must,
            As chimney sweepers, come to dust."

Blackout.

ACT II

Scene 5

*Late that night. A dimly lit room in the
home of Duplass. A bottle and glasses on
a table. Duplass sits drinking. Lacoste
enters and pours himself a drink.*

Lacoste. Duplass. Forbear, my friend.
    (He takes a deep swallow of his drink.)
O pardon me for bringing this ill news;
    (Takes another swallow.)
I am loath to tell you.

Duplass. (Startled, rising.) Dead? Already?
  Would they not wait for execution in the morn?

Lacoste. As 'tis reported, she did with desp'rate hand
  Fordo her own life.

Duplass. By heaven! But yesterday I spoke with her!
  So with herself was she in mutiny.
  The Lord protect her! she's gone; she's dead!

Lacoste. Betrayed to fortune by foul corruption.
  Why should the private pleasure of some one—
  One man's lust—so many lives confound?

Duplass. The sweet'st, dear'st creature's dead: and
      vengeance for't
  Not dropp'd down yet.
  Thou hast made me giddy with these ill tidings.

Lacoste. She should have died hereafter:
    I shall not look upon her like again.

Duplass. Let this pernicious hour
    Stand aye accursed in the calendar!
    Methinks it should be now some huge eclipse
    Of sun and moon, and that the affrighted globe
    Should yawn at alteration.

Lacoste. A joyless, dismal, black, and sorrowful issue.
    (Takes a deep breath and draws his jacket
    close.)
    'Tis bitter cold, and I am sick at heart.

Duplass. My grief's so great it boundeth where it falls,
    Not with empty hollowness, but weight,
    And no supporter but the huge firm earth
    Can hold it up:
    Nor can my tongue unload my heart's great
        burden;
    For selfsame wind that I should speak withal
    Is kindling coals that fires all my breast.

Lacoste. Weep I cannot, but my heart bleeds;
    Mine eyes are turn'd to fire.

Duplass. I forbid my tears.
    (Begins to weep.)
    But yet it is our trick; nature her custom holds,
    Let shame say what it will.

Lacoste. It is no shame.

Duplass. (Amid his sobs.) I honor'd her, I lov'd her,
    and will weep
    My date of life out for her sweet life's loss;

These tears are my sweet sister's obsequies,
And every drop cries vengeance for her death.

Lacoste. God will revenge it; whom I will importune
With daily prayers.

Duplass. The dismall'st day is this that e'er I saw.
All's cheerless, dark, and deadly. From this instant,
There's nothing serious in mortality.

Blackout.

ACT II

Scene 6

*Later yet that night. A dark bed chamber.
Arnaud sits in a chair, unseen. Sound of a
door opening and footsteps. Enter Contessa
unseen, in the dark.*

Contessa. (Softly.) Sleepest or wakest thou, Father?

> *Arnaud switches on a table lamp that
> barely illuminates the room.*

Arnaud. I have been broad awake two hours and more.
In my heart there was a kind of fighting
That would not let me sleep. In a dream,
Methought I heard a voice cry "sleep no more."

Contessa. 'T has been turbulent and stormy.

Arnaud. Nor heaven nor earth have been at peace;
The obscure bird clamor'd the livelong night;
Would it were day. Why do you stir so early?

Contessa. I can tell you strange news that you yet
dreamt
Not of: Lady Martine is dead.

Arnaud. No.
(His chin falling to his chest.)
No.

(Shaking his head after a very long pause.)
Dead, then?

Contessa. Dead.

Arnaud. How ended she?

Contessa. By self and violent hands she took off her life.
     I lay the blame upon her own despair.

Arnaud. My soul is full of discord and dismay.

Contessa. (Brightly.) But you have prevailed.

Arnaud. Do you triumph, Tessa? Is this winning?
     Hath thy fiery heart so parch'd thine entrails
     That not a tear can fall for poor Martine?
     I did not think to be so sad tonight
     As this hath made me.
     Look thee, how inly sorrow gripes my soul.
     What our contempts doth often hurl from us,
     We wish it ours again; she's good, being gone.
     Whilst I remember her and her virtues,
     I cannot forget my blemishes.

Contessa. Do as the heavens have done, forget your
          evil;
     With them, forgive yourself.

Arnaud. She should have lived; I did her wrong,
     And here abjure the taints and blames
     I laid upon Martine.
          (Pause.)
     I meant to stay the judgment
     And reverse the doom of death;
     To extenuate rather than enforce
     The sentence: I did intend to pardon her.

There's a great spirit gone! Thus did I desire it:
And for this sin there is no remedy.
Our natures do pursue,
Like rats that ravin down their proper bane,
A thirsty evil; and when we drink, we die.

Contessa. Woe that too late repents, Monsieur
        Remorse;
    The lady is dead upon your accusations.

Arnaud. (Stridently.) Ay, this is so! She I kill'd! but
        thou strikest me
    Sorely, to say I did; it is as bitter
    Upon thy tongue as in my thought: now, good now,
    Say so but seldom.

Contessa. What's gone and what's past help should be
        past grief.

Arnaud. I could give better comfort than you do.

Contessa. The point is this: an end, and that is all.

Arnaud. Oh, were that all!
    This must be answer'd, either here or hence.

Contessa. (Annoyed.) Look, what is done cannot be
        now amended;
    Forget this grief.

Arnaud. Teach me to forget myself! Speak no more!
    Thou turn'st my eyes into my very soul,
    And there I see such black and grained spots
    As will not leave their tinct. I have done ill,
    Of which I do accuse myself so sorely
    That I will joy no more. O, Martine!
    The wrongs I have done thee stir afresh within me;

Forgive my tyranny; forgive my sins!
I have deserv'd all tongues to talk their bitt'rest!
Arnaud, thou tyrant! therefore betake thee
To nothing but despair.

Contessa. (Sarcastically.) How smart a lash that
    speech doth give thy conscience.

Arnaud. Yea, I mean to rectify my conscience!

Contessa. What's done is done. Things without all
    remedy
Should be without regard.

Arnaud. Hadst thou but shook thy head or made a
    pause
When I spake darkly what I purposed,
Or turn'd an eye of doubt upon my face—

Contessa. Say no more!

Arnaud. —Deep shame had struck me dumb, made me
    break off,
But, without stop, thou didst let thy heart consent.

Contessa. Enough!

Arnaud. Ay! You stared upon me with ungentle looks
    And urged me further; nay, urg'd extremely for't!

Contessa. Not one word more of the consumed time!

Arnaud. Truly, the souls of men are full of dread.
    And what's to come of my despised time
    Is naught but bitterness.
    Nature seems dead; and wicked dreams abuse
    The curtain'd sleep. Of comfort no man speak:

By heaven, I'll hate him everlastingly
That bids me be of comfort anymore.
Let there be no noise made, dear Contessa,
Unless some dull and favorable hand
Will whisper music to my weary spirit.

Contessa. Martine is dead; there is no more to say.

Arnaud. You understand me not that tell me so.

Curtain.

THE END.